Activities
for the
Internet

An Introduction

Joyce Perkins
Hardin-Jefferson High School
Sour Lake, Texas

Dr. Joe Jernigan, Assistant Professor of Educational Technology
The University of Texas at Arlington
Arlington, Texas

Reviewers:

Kay Franklin
Canyon High School
New Braunfels, Texas

Kay Cade Pleasant
Tyler ISD
Tyler, Texas

Jamye Swinford
Crane High School
Crane, Texas

JOIN US ON THE INTERNET
WWW: http://www.thomson.com
EMAIL: findit@kiosk.thomson.com   A service of I(T)P®

South-Western Educational Publishing
an International Thomson Publishing company I(T)P®

Cincinnati • Albany, NY • Belmont, CA • Bonn • Boston • Detroit • Johannesburg • London • Madrid
Melbourne • Mexico City • New York • Paris • Singapore • Tokyo • Toronto • Washington

Managing Editor: Janie F. Schwark
Editor: Becky E. Peveler
Marketing Manager: John Wills
Development Services: FSCreations, Inc.
Production Services: FSCreations, Inc. and Mary Hartkemeyer
Internal/Cover Design: Ann Small
Internal/Cover Photo: Marjory Dressler
Manufacturing Coordinator: Mardell Toomey

ITP

South-Western Educational Publishing is a division of International Thomson Publishing, Inc. The ITP logo is a registered trademark used herein under license by South-Western Educational Publishing.

Preface

Our lives continue to change in many ways with the tremendous impact of the Internet, the World Wide Web, and telecommunications. Business we once handled by visits, calls, or mail to stores and offices, we now conduct on the computer via the Internet. The Internet has a wealth of information that you can access from a classroom, your home, or work. And you can communicate with anyone around the world when you learn to use the Internet.

Activities for the Internet: An Introduction will guide you each step of the way in your exploration of the Internet. After exploring the Internet for just a very few hours, you will be comfortable with how to access information and thus be better prepared for the twenty-first century. Your journey will provide educational experiences, challenges, and excitement; new friendships; and new knowledge and skills for success at school, at work, and at home.

ORGANIZATION OF THE BOOK

Activities for the Internet: An Introduction is divided into three parts:

Part 1—Introduction

Part 1 provides an overview of the primary tools for exploring the Internet. You will be introduced to the basic terminology related to the Internet and the World Wide Web. Whether you will be using Netscape Navigator or Microsoft Internet Explorer, you will find the step-by-step instructions to help you learn how to explore on the Internet. After you complete the Introduction, you will be ready to explore on your own in the activities.

Part 2—Activities

Part 2 has thirty independent Internet activities, organized from the simple to the more complicated. The activities provide steps to guide you as you explore the Internet. As you complete each activity, you will have an opportunity to:

- Learn and apply telecommunications skills.
- Gain new knowledge about personal, local, state, national, and international business topics.
- Develop critical thinking, communication, and teamwork skills as you apply emerging technologies in personal and workplace business situations.

Part 3—Glossary

Part 3 lists terms and definitions to help you expand your vocabulary. Access the glossary whenever you need to review the definition of an Internet-related term that you may have seen elsewhere in the book.

FEATURES OF THE BOOK

Take time now to notice these features in *Activities for the Internet: An Introduction*:

- **Net Web Wisdom,** in the form of marginal notes throughout the book, provides answers to FAQs about the Internet and the World Wide Web.
- **Notes** provide hints to help you explore successfully.
- **Screen illustrations** that you may encounter on your journey are included. Because the Internet is ever-changing, some of the screen illustrations may look different on your screen.
- **Objectives** identify what you should learn during your exploration for each activity.
- **Feedback questions** in each of the thirty activities guide your exploration.
- **Applications** within each activity direct you to create documents using word processing, spreadsheet, database, telecommunications, desktop publishing, presentation, and other applications software.

ACKNOWLEDGMENTS

Writing this book was truly a team effort. Our many thanks to:

- Becky Peveler, our developmental editor at South-Western Educational Publishing, who believed in us through this fast and furious project.
- Nina Watson, our editor at FSCreations, Inc., who did an extraordinary job of deciphering our e-mail and learning along with us. Because of the capability of telecommunications, almost all our work was sent to one another via e-mail.

Special thanks to our reviewers for their contributions:

- Kay Franklin, Canyon High School, New Braunfels, Texas
- Kay Cade Pleasant, Tyler ISD, Tyler, Texas
- Jamye Swinford, Crane High School, Crane, Texas

Finally, from Joyce, a huge hug to my family: Mark and Justin. Even though I was busy with all the other things at home, at school, or with student council, my family supported me throughout the work on this project. Also a big thanks for the years of support to my extended online family and my colleagues at Lesley College and Hardin-Jefferson High School.

From Joe, thanks to those who had to put up with me during this project: my best friend, Archie Bailey; my colleagues at The University of Texas at Arlington; and the one who sacrificed most of his time with me, my dog Ed Earl.

We welcome an e-mail message to let us know your reactions to this book or your thoughts about your favorite activity. You may send an e-mail message to either of us at these addresses:

Joyce Perkins   jperkins@tenet.edu
Joe Jernigan   joej@tenet.edu or jernigan@uta.edu

As you explore the Internet, concentrate on learning all you can about the world of telecommunications. As a result, you will acquire knowledge and technical skills for success at school, at work, and at home.

Joyce Perkins
Joe Jernigan

Contents

Part 3   Glossary   **109**

Index   **117**

Acknowledgments

For permission to reproduce the screen captures on the indicated pages, acknowledgment is made to the following:

Page	Source
7, 15, 26, 32, 50, 83	Netscape Communications Corporation has not authorized, sponsored, or endorsed, or approved this publication and is not responsible for its content. Netscape and the Netscape Communications Corporate Logos, are trademarks and trade names of Netscape Communications Corporation. All other product names and/or logos are trademarks of their respective owners.
8, 26, 32	Microsoft Corporation has not authorized, sponsored, or endorsed, or approved this publication and is not responsible for its content. Microsoft is a registered trademark of Microsoft Corporation.
7, 9, 55	U.S. Census Bureau
29	Central Intelligence Agency
34	The Weather Channel
37	The Purdue University On-line Writing Lab
40	U.S. Department of State
42	The National Park Service: ParkNet
48	National Association of Secondary Schools Principals
52	*Computer Shopper* and Ziff-Davis Publishing Company
58	RealTime Quotes
63	Bates College Online
66	SunSITE
68	Insurance News Network
71	The Toronto-Dominion Bank Web Site
77	Adobe and Adobe Acrobat are trademarks of Adobe Systems Incorporated.

Page	Source
80	The Clip Art Connection
86	Used with permission of the American National Red Cross, copyright 1996.
92	Deja News
96	National Center for Supercomputing Applications at the University of Illinois
98	*USA Today* online site
104	Project Gutenberg
107	3Com

JOIN US ON THE INTERNET

WWW: **http://www.thomson.com**
E-MAIL: **findit@kiosk.thomson.com**

South-Western Educational Publishing is a partner in *thomson.com*, an on-line portal for the products, services, and resources available from International Thomson Publishing (ITP). Through our site, users can search catalogs, examine subject-specific resource centers, and subscribe to electronic discussion lists.

South-Western Educational Publishing is also a reseller of commercial software products. See our printed catalog or view this page at:

http://www.swpco.com/swpco/comp_ed/com_sft.html

For information on our products visit our World Wide Web site at:

http://www.swpco.com/swpco.html

To join the South-Western Computer Education discussion list, send an e-mail message to: **majordomo@list.thomson.com**. Leave the subject field blank, and in the body of your message key: SUBSCRIBE SOUTH-WESTERN-COMPUTER-EDUCATION <your e-mail address>.

A service of I(T)P®

One Two Three

1 2 3

Introduction

▶ OVERVIEW

Do you remember when you made a phone call to communicate with someone, you placed a stamp on your mail, you went to a library to conduct research, you visited a retail store to shop for clothing or books, you visited a travel agency to arrange a trip, or you learned about the weather by listening to weather reports?

Why is the Internet so important to the world?

Now our world is so very different. You can conduct much of your daily business on the computer. E-mail addresses and World Wide Web sites are everywhere: in newspapers, magazines, and journals; on business cards and letterhead; on television and radio commercials; on billboards; on the local and national news; and on junk mail. Many of your friends may even have an e-mail address.

What is the Internet?

Your teacher will discuss the communications software you will be using.

You have undoubtedly heard about the Internet, the information superhighway, or surfing the Net. The Internet, also called the Net, consists of people, information, and millions of interconnected computer networks throughout the world. Most businesses and homes are connected to the Internet via an **Internet service provider** (ISP) such as America Online, CompuServe, Prodigy, or a local provider. For a monthly fee, an ISP will provide full Internet access through a phone line. All you need is a computer, communications software, and a modem with a phone line.

If you have ever been to a library, you have seen the physical equivalent of the Internet. A library contains thousands of books, each stored on a specific shelf in a specific section of the library. Each book has a unique number, or address, assigned to it that tells you exactly where you can find the book. Each item on the Internet also has a unique address that allows you to access specific files.

Your browser will help you find information on the Internet

Special software programs called **browsers** help you find information on the Internet. Since the information on the Internet is **hypertext-driven**, you can jump from a word, graphic, or phrase to another section in a document or to a different document via a **hypertext link**.

Internet Addresses

When you are connected to the Internet, you are identified by a unique address. This address allows you to access information, and others may send information to your address. An Internet address may be numeric, alphabetic, or a combination of numbers and letters. Internet e-mail addresses always use lowercase letters with no spaces.

All Internet e-mail addresses have several parts, separated by the @ (pronounced *at*) symbol. The **username** identifies the specific person at that site. The **domain** and **subdomain** identify the computer where the user is working. The last three letters, called the **domain extension** or the **top-level domain**, refer to the top domain name for the network. Common domain extensions are shown in Figure 1-1 on page 4.

Figure 1-1
Common Domain
Extensions

Domain Extension	Description	Example of Internet Address
.com	Commercial Service	billg@microsoft.com (Bill Gates, CEO of Microsoft Corporation)
.edu	Education or Education-related Organization	jperkins@tenet.edu (Joyce Perkins, a coauthor of this text)
.gov	Government	president@whitehouse.gov (The President of the United States)
.mil	Military	shorta@karpeles.ims.disa.mil (General Alonzo Short, head of the Defense Information Systems Agency)
.net	Network Provider	@fuse.net (an Internet service provider via Cincinnati Bell Telephone)
.org	Organization	@nassp.org (National Association of Secondary School Principals)

Each hypertext link has a unique URL.

Files on the Internet have a similar kind of location number, or address, called a **Universal Resource Locator**, or **URL** (pronounced *Earl*). Each hypertext link is connected to a unique URL, telling the browser where to find that particular document. URL names look different than normal Internet names. These long names are seen everywhere in hyperspace. The following are some examples:

http://www.disney.com/	Disneyland
http://www.whitehouse.gov/	White House
http://cdsweb.u-strasbg.fr/~heck/sf.htm/	The Star's Family of Astronomy
http://fi-www.arc.nasa.gov/fia/projects/ bayes-group/Atlas/Mars/	Atlas of Mars

Many URLs begin with http:.

You must type the URL exactly correct, with no spaces in the address. Since URLs are also case sensitive, you must type uppercase or lowercase letters exactly as shown.

What is the World Wide Web?

The **World Wide Web**, also known as the WWW, is a hypermedia system that lets you browse through lots of information on the Internet. You can find information on just about any topic. If you enter the URL for the information you want to access on the Internet, your browser will jump or **link** immediately to that location. Or, from a browser, you can jump easily from a hypertext link in one document to another page in the same document or to a different site and other documents all over the world. By exploring link after link, you create a web of connections.

Will you be using a graphical browser or a text browser?

A **graphical browser** (often called a GUI or a graphical user interface and pronounced *gooey*) allows you to access text, color, video, sound, and multimedia presentations on the Internet. Popular graphical browsers are Netscape Navigator (or Netscape) and Microsoft Internet Explorer (or Explorer). A **text browser**, such as Lynx, provides access to only text (or words) on the Internet. To access graphics or pictures using Lynx, you must download the pages and then use a graphics viewer.

The hypertext links on home pages and web pages are highlighted, underlined, or in a different color.

Documents on the World Wide Web are referred to as either home pages or web pages. A **home page** is the main page for a web site. You can compare a home page to a menu, since the home page will often identify links to other pages at this site. A **web page** (or **page**) contains the information for a hypertext link. Home pages and web pages may have numerous links. As an example, Disneyland has only one home page (**http://www.disney.com**) with many hypertext links, each with a unique URL (such as the Disney Store at **http://store.disney.com/** or Disney Publishing at **http://www.disney.com/DisneyBooks/**).

Some HTML documents have *.html* or *.htm* at the end of the URL.

With the variety of computer applications, all documents are not created the same way. For example, some documents could have been created using WordPerfect, while others may be in Microsoft Word. Some documents are in a DOS format, while others are Macintosh documents. For everyone in the world to read each other's files, HTML was developed. **HTML**, or HyperText Markup Language, refers to the embedded instructions within regular text. These instructions allow each browser to display a document clearly on your screen.

Tips for Getting Started

To help you learn about the Internet, follow these tips:

- Log on to the Internet daily.
- Schedule an uninterrupted block of time to explore.
- Be responsible for acceptable computer use and for your teacher's account.

Responsible behavior is critical when you access the Internet. Your teacher will discuss the acceptable use policy you must follow.

- Keep a pen or pencil and a spiral notebook or notepad nearby to record important information.
- Get into the habit of keeping a journal of your online activities, critical commands or steps you most often use, and e-mail addresses of users with whom you would like to communicate.
- After you are off-line, get into the habit of reviewing what you learned during that session.
- Always prepare for your next online session. Think about where you will want to try to find the information you are looking for or how you can make your online session more productive.

The Introduction will help you get started using the Internet.

As you complete the activities in this book, you will become comfortable with the Internet. Your journey will provide educational experiences, challenges, and excitement; new friendships; and new knowledge and skills for success at school, at work, and at home. You will learn how to use the Internet to gain information about the diverse cultures of the world, to conduct research, to try software, to communicate with others, to arrange travel plans, to discuss your favorite topic, to look at fashion designs before they arrive at your local department store, to explore the world, and on and on.

By now you should be familiar with terms such as Internet, ISP, browsers, hypertext link, address, URL, WWW, graphical browser, text browser, HTML, home page, *and* web page (*or* page). *If you aren't, please review the material on pages 3–6 before you begin working at the computer in the next section.*

▶ LAUNCHING YOUR BROWSER

Remember that your browser helps you find information on the Internet. The steps to launch your browser will vary with the communications software that you will be using. No matter what communications software you will use, however, you will learn quickly as part of your daily routine how to launch your browser.

Important: The step-by-step instructions in this book are based on Netscape Navigator 3.0 and Microsoft Internet Explorer 3.0. If you are using an earlier or more recent version of the software, some steps may differ depending on the activity.

If you are using Netscape Navigator for Windows or for a Macintosh computer, follow these steps to launch your browser:

1. Start the Netscape Navigator software. The Netscape Navigator home page will appear unless you set a different start page. If the Netscape Navigator home page did not appear, type **http://home.netscape.com/** in the Location box.
   Note: The Location box is located near the top of the window. The name of the box changes when your browser links to sites. You will see these names for the Location box: *Netsite:, Go to:,* and *Location.*

2. Your screen should be similar to the Netscape Navigator home page in Figure 1-2 on page 7. Realize that the content on a web page may change at any time.

   The **status indicator** at the bottom of the screen animates to show the progress of the current operation. The URLs for each hypertext link will appear in this area. The **toolbar buttons** at the top of the screen activate Netscape Navigator features. Click on the buttons to revisit pages, reload pages, load images, open locations, print pages, find text, and stop transfers in progress. The **directory buttons** under the toolbar buttons bring pages whose information helps you browse the Internet, such as new sites and "cool" sites.

3. Because most documents are larger than what appears on your screen, use the scroll bar to move up and down the pages to read the entire document.
   Note: Get into the habit of scrolling the home page of each site you visit so you will know the hypertext links on the home page.

4. In the Location box, type **http://www.census.gov/** and press ENTER/ RETURN. You will be connected to the web page for the U.S. Census Bureau as shown in Figure 1-3 on page 7.

Since all graphical browsers have similar features, you will be able to use different browsers after you learn about Netscape Navigator or Microsoft Internet Explorer.

Netscape

Practice these steps to become comfortable with launching Netscape Navigator and linking to other pages and sites. When you are ready to exit Netscape Navigator, see "Exiting Your Computer Session" on page 22.

Figure 1-2
Netscape Navigator Home Page

Toolbar Buttons

Directory Buttons

Hypertext Link

Status Indicator

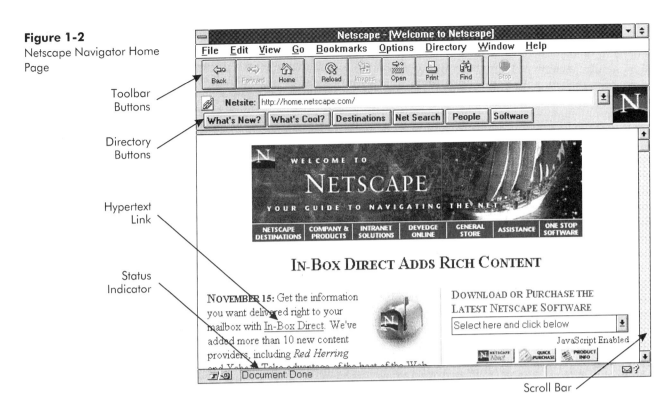

Figure 1-3
U.S. Census Bureau Home Page from Netscape

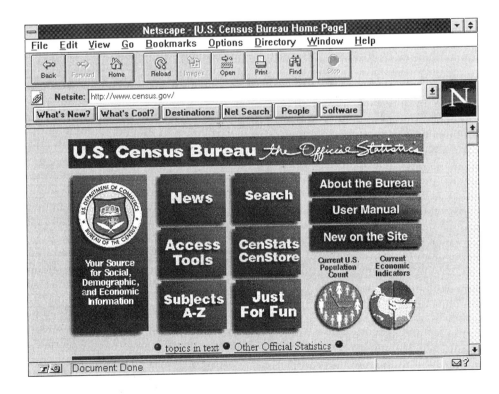

Important: As you explore the Internet, always remember to leave an objectionable site quickly by clicking the Home button. You will immediately return to the home page set up for your browser.

5. *Optional:* Click on the Print button to print the home page that appears on your screen.
   Note: The default is set to print all the pages in the document, but you can specify the pages that you want to print in the Print dialog box.

6. Read the U.S. Census Bureau home page, and click on any hypertext link.

7. Practice using hypertext by selecting several more links.

8. Click on the Back button, and retrace your steps until you reach the U.S. Census Bureau home page.

9. Click on the Forward button to retrace the links you chose earlier.

10. Click the Home button to go to the Netscape Navigator home page.

Explorer

Practice these steps to become comfortable with launching Explorer and linking to other pages and sites. When you are ready to exit the browser, see "Exiting Your Computer Session" on page 22.

If you are using Microsoft Internet Explorer for Windows or for a Macintosh computer, follow these steps to launch your browser:

1. Start the Microsoft Internet Explorer software. The Microsoft Internet Explorer home page will appear unless you set a different start page. If the Explorer home page did not appear, type **http://home.microsoft.com/** in the Address box near the top of the window.

2. Your screen should be similar to the Microsoft Internet Explorer home page in Figure 1-4. Realize that the content on a web page may change at any time.

Figure 1-4
Microsoft Internet Explorer
Home Page

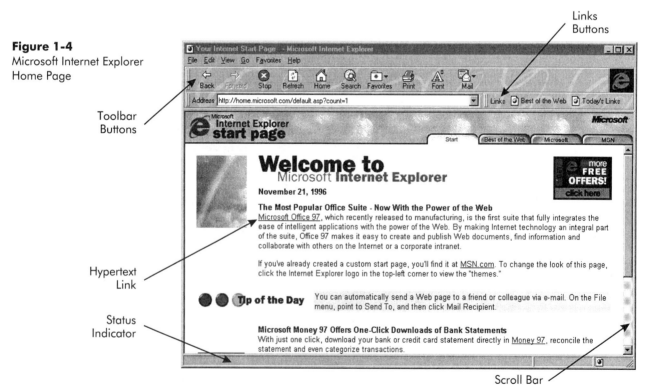

The **status indicator** at the bottom of the screen animates to show the progress of the current operation. The URLs for each hypertext link will appear in this area. The **toolbar buttons** at the top of the screen activate Explorer features. Click on the buttons to revisit pages, refresh pages, load images, open locations, print pages, search for text, and stop transfers in progress. The **links buttons** next to the Address box bring pages whose information helps you browse the Internet, such as "Best of the Web" and "Today's Links."

3. Because most documents are larger than what appears on your screen, use the scroll bar to move up and down the pages to read the entire document.
   Note: Get into the habit of scrolling the home page of each site you visit so you will know the hypertext links on the home page.

4. In the Address box, type **http://www.census.gov/** and press ENTER/ RETURN. You will be connected to the web page for the U.S. Census Bureau as shown in Figure 1-5.

Figure 1-5
U.S. Census Bureau Home
Page from Explorer

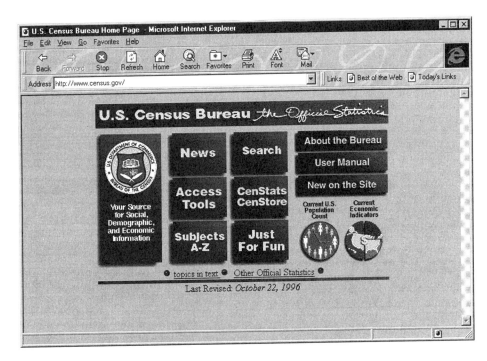

Important: As you explore the Internet, always remember to leave an objectionable site quickly by clicking the Home button. You will immediately return to the home page set up for your browser.

5. *Optional:* Click on the Print button to print the home page that appears on your screen.
   Note: The default is set to print all the pages in the document, but you can specify the pages that you want to print in the Print dialog box.

6. Read the U.S. Census Bureau home page, and click on any hypertext link.

7. Practice using hypertext by selecting several more links.

8. Click on the Back button, and retrace your steps until you reach the U.S. Census Bureau home page.

9. Click on the Forward button to retrace the links you chose earlier.

10. Click the Home button to go to the Internet Explorer home page.

ACCESSING ONLINE HELP

Whenever you need to learn or review the steps to perform various tasks, you can access online help. Online help provides definitions, instructions, and perhaps a tutorial to help you become familiar with the functions of the software.

Netscape

If you are using Netscape Navigator, follow these steps to access online help:

1. If you need help at any time when you are using Netscape Navigator, choose the **Help** menu. Note the various options.

2. To access descriptions of terms and instructions to perform a specific task, choose *Handbook*.

3. Scroll down the page. Explore the tutorial options if you want to review the basics of Netscape Navigator. If you want to search for help on a particular topic, continue scrolling to the *Index*. By choosing the initial letter of the topic in which you need help, Netscape Navigator will link immediately to the items in the Index. Continue using hypertext links to find the information you need.

4. To exit Help and to continue browsing, click on the Back button or choose to go to a specific page.

Explorer

If you are using Microsoft Internet Explorer, follow these steps to access online help:

1. If you need help at any time when you are using Explorer, choose the **Help** menu. Note the various options.

2. To access descriptions of terms and instructions to perform a specific task, choose *Help Topics*. If you want to search for help on a particular topic, continue scrolling through the list. Click on a topic about which you want to learn more.

3. Choose *Web Tutorial* if you want to review the basics of Explorer or if you want to complete lessons. Go to URL: **http://www.msn.com/ tutorial/default.html** if the *Web Tutorial* is not available in the **Help** menu. Continue using hypertext links to find the information you need.

4. To exit Help and to continue browsing, click on the Back button or choose to go to a specific page.

FINDING FILES WITH SEARCH ENGINES

When you don't know a specific URL for the information you need, you can use a search engine. A **search engine** allows you to search for information on a particular topic on the Internet. For example, you could search for the words *space shuttle*. A search engine will access the Internet and show you a list of documents containing the words *space* and *shuttle*. You would then browse the documents to find the information that interests you. Examples of popular search engines are Yahoo, AltaVista, Lycos, Magellan, and Excite. In addition, some sites have their own search engine to help you locate information within their site.

Netscape

Practice these steps to use a search engine. When you are ready to exit Netscape Navigator, see "Exiting Your Computer Session" on page 22.

If you are using Netscape Navigator, follow these steps to use a search engine:

1. Click on the Net Search directory button, and choose one of the search engines that appear on your screen.
   Note: Net Search allows you to link to numerous search engines; scroll to the end of this page to choose a search engine. You may also go directly to a particular search engine immediately after you launch your browser by typing the URL for the desired search engine in the Location box. For example, you can type **http://www.yahoo.com/** in the Location box and press ENTER/RETURN. Netscape Navigator will take you directly to the Yahoo home page.

2. In the search text box, type **white house**, and click on the Search button. Netscape Navigator will begin the searching process.
   Note: You may need to scroll down the page to locate the search text box.

The results of your search may include links to information all over the world.

3. Netscape Navigator will display the search results. Explore the links that interest you.
   Note: Be aware that searching at different times may bring different results. You can print a page by clicking on the Print button from your browser, or you can save a page by choosing *Save As* from the **File** menu.

4. When you find a page that you like, you can create a bookmark and let Netscape Navigator keep track of the URL. Go now to a web page that you like.

A bookmark flags the location of a document. You can create as many bookmarks as you want.

5. From the **Bookmarks** menu, choose *Add Bookmark*. You just marked this page for future use. Netscape Navigator will remember the URL and display the name of the document in your list of bookmarks.

6. You can easily access your bookmarks by choosing the **Bookmarks** menu. Then scroll through the list to find the page you want to visit. Within seconds, Netscape Navigator will link to the page.
   Note: To delete a bookmark, choose the *Go to Bookmark* option, highlight the bookmark in the list, and press DELETE.

7. Return to the Netscape Navigator home page.

Explorer

Practice these steps to use a search engine. When you are ready to exit Microsoft Internet Explorer, see "Exiting Your Computer Session" on page 22.

If you are using Microsoft Internet Explorer, follow these steps to use a search engine:

1. Click the Search button on the Toolbar.
   Note: The Search option allows you to link to numerous search engines from a single page. You may also go directly to a particular search engine immediately after you launch your browser by typing the URL for the desired search engine in the Address box. For example, you may type **http://www.yahoo.com/** in the Address box and press ENTER/RETURN. Internet Explorer will take you directly to the Yahoo home page.

2. In the search text box, type **white house,** and click on the Search button. Microsoft Internet Explorer will begin the searching process.

3. Your browser will display the search results. Explore the links that interest you.
   Note: Be aware that searching at different times may bring different results. You can print a page by clicking on the Print button from your browser, or you can save a page by choosing *Save As* from the **File** menu.

4. When you find a page that you like, you can create a bookmark and let Microsoft Internet Explorer keep track of the URL. Go now to a web page that you like.

5. From the **Favorites** menu, choose *Add to Favorites.* You just marked this page for future use. Microsoft Internet Explorer will remember the URL and display the name of the document in your list of favorites.

6. You can easily access your favorite pages by choosing the **Favorites** menu or by clicking the Favorites button. Then scroll through the list to find the page you want to visit. Within seconds, Microsoft Internet Explorer will link to the page.
   Note: To delete a bookmark, choose *Organize Favorites* from the **Favorites** menu. Highlight the bookmark you want to remove, and click the Delete button.

7. Return to the Microsoft Internet Explorer home page.

▶ ACCESSING GOPHER SITES

Gopher is a menu-based tool that allows you to search millions of directories and databases of text documents throughout the Internet. When you access gopher sites, you navigate from one menu to another menu and to submenus by choosing menu items until you find information that interests you. Gopher menus are usually very plain, with only hypertext links. If you find a menu or page that you may want to visit again, remember to add a bookmark. The URL for a gopher site begins with **gopher://.**

Netscape

If you are using Netscape Navigator, follow these steps to access gopher sites:

1. Go to the Library of Congress' Marvel gopher site at this URL: **gopher://marvel.loc.gov/**

2. Review the hypertext links on the gopher menu, and choose *Copyright.*
   Note: With gopher, you will dig through menus and more menus.

3. Another gopher menu will appear. Choose *Copyright Basics.* After digging through two menus, you now have a page on your screen to read.
   Note: Realize that searching at different times may bring different results; add a bookmark when you find a page you want to revisit. You can print a page by clicking on the Print button, or you can save a file by choosing *Save As* from the **File** menu.

4. Click on the Back button to review the menus and explore for other pages that interest you.

Explorer

The URL for a gopher site begins with **gopher:**.

If you are using Microsoft Internet Explorer, follow these steps to access gopher sites:

1. Go to the Library of Congress' Marvel gopher site at this URL: **gopher://marvel.loc.gov/**

2. Review the hypertext links on the gopher menu, and choose *Copyright*. *Note:* With gopher, you will dig through menus and more menus.

3. Another gopher menu will appear. Choose *Copyright Basics*. After digging through two menus, you now have a page on your screen to read. *Note:* Realize that searching at different times may bring different results; add a bookmark when you find a page you want to revisit. You can print a page by clicking on the Print button, or you can save a file by choosing *Save As* from the **File** menu.

4. Click on the Back button to review the menus and explore for other pages that interest you.

▶ RETRIEVING FTP FILES

You can use your browser to access FTP files.

One of the most popular uses of the Internet is the ability to **download** (or retrieve and copy) files from one computer to another. **File Transfer Protocol**, or FTP, was devised to retrieve a file that is on a computer located anywhere on the Internet. FTP files include freeware or shareware programs, publications, clip art, and many others.

The URL for an FTP site begins with **ftp:**.

FTP web pages are usually very plain, with only hypertext links and information about the files. For some FTP files, such as text documents, you can download the file and display it immediately on your screen. Other documents (for example, word processing, spreadsheet, or database) may have to be downloaded and then opened by running the appropriate program. For example, to open an Excel spreadsheet, you must have the Microsoft Excel software. For software programs, you must download such FTP files directly to a file on your hard drive. Then you may have to uncompress the file before you can run the program.

Netscape

If you are using Netscape Navigator, follow these steps to retrieve an FTP file:

1. Go to the Library of Congress FTP site at this URL: **ftp://ftp.loc.gov/pub/**

2. Notice the Folder (directory) and Document icons. Click on a directory icon to display a new list of files. *Note:* Notice the hypertext link Up to higher level directory at the beginning of the list. If you explored, click on this link to return to the */pub/* directory.

3. Link to the *README* file. A document called "Library of Congress Files Available through FTP" will appear on your screen.

Before you download a program file to a school computer, ask permission from your teacher. Then to avoid contaminating your computer, always run a virus checker on the file.

4. From the **File** menu, choose *Save As*. Then verify the directory (folder) and drive where you want to save the file.

5. Type **ftpinfo** for the file name, and save the file to disk.

Explorer

If you are using Microsoft Internet Explorer, follow these steps to retrieve an FTP file:

1. Go to the Library of Congress FTP site at this URL: **ftp://ftp.loc.gov/pub/**

2. Click on a directory name to display a new list of files.
   Note: Notice the hypertext link <u>Up to higher level directory</u> at the beginning of the list. If you explored, click on this link to return to the */pub/* directory.

3. Link to the *README* file. A document called "Library of Congress Files Available through FTP" will appear on your screen.

4. From the **File** menu, choose *Save As*. Then verify the directory (folder) and drive where you want to save the file.

5. Type **ftpinfo** for the file name, and save the file to disk.

> Before you download a program file to a school computer, ask permission from your teacher. Then to avoid contaminating your computer, always run a virus checker on the file.

COMMUNICATING WITH OTHERS

You can communicate with others who are connected to the Internet through e-mail communications, mailing lists, and news and conference areas. Because no one governs the Internet in terms of behavior and ethics, you should practice basic **netiquette**, or network etiquette, in all your e-mail communications. Consider these basic netiquette guidelines:

> Practice basic netiquette in all your communications.

- Always use a subject line in each e-mail message. This will allow the receiver to glance quickly at the e-mail message and have an idea of the topic of the message.

- Limit each e-mail message to one subject.

- Write clear, concise messages.

- Use upper- and lowercase letters in your messages.

- Use correct spelling, grammar, and punctuation.

- Use emoticons with caution. As shown in the following examples, an **emoticon** is a combination of symbols and letters that when combined display a little picture that expresses an emotion when you tilt your head to the left side.

:-)	smiling	;-o	Oh My!
;-}	laughing while winking	: - (	sad

- Use abbreviations as appropriate. Here are a few common abbreviations:
  BTW   by the way
  BRB   be right back
  GMTA   great minds think alike
  FYI   for your information

- Watch the tone of your message. Your word choice and how you explain things will determine the tone of your message.

- Always include your name (or signature) at the end of each message.

> Be responsible for understanding and following your school's computer use policy.

- Always communicate in a responsible manner. Realize that the receiver may share your message with others. And also realize that once you send your message, you cannot take it back.

Using Your E-Mail Software

Technically known as **electronic mail**, e-mail is the transfer of information in electronic format. With e-mail you will be able to send messages to and receive messages from anyone in the world who has an e-mail address whenever you want. As shown in Figure 1-6, an e-mail message has a heading, body, and signature.

Figure 1-6
Message Composition
Window with Netscape
Navigator Mail

Heading

Body

Signature

```
┌─────────────────────── Netscape - [Message Composition] ──────────────────┐
│  File   Edit   View   Options   Window                                  N  │
│  ┌──────┐ ┌──────┐ ┌──────┐ ┌───────┐ ┌──────┐                            │
│  │ Send │ │Quote │ │Attach│ │Address│ │ Stop │                            │
│  ┌─────────────┐ ┌─────────────────────────────────────────────┐          │
│  │   Mail To:  │ │ jernigan@imagin.net                         │          │
│  ┌─────────────┐ ┌─────────────────────────────────────────────┐          │
│  │     Cc:     │ │ jperkins@tenet.edu                          │          │
│  ┌─────────────┐ ┌─────────────────────────────────────────────┐          │
│  │   Subject:  │ │ Internet Seminar                            │          │
│  ┌─────────────┐ ┌─────────────────────────────────────────────┐          │
│  │ Attachment: │ │                                             │          │
│  Joe, have you heard about the Internet seminar on November 20 at The University of │
│  Cincinnati? Nationally-recognized speakers will present the latest information about │
│  using the Internet. Are you interested in more information about the seminar? │
│                                                                            │
│  Rebecca Smith                                                             │
│                                                                            │
│  Netscape                                                                  │
└────────────────────────────────────────────────────────────────────────────┘
```

Before you use your e-mail software, access online help to read about the features of your software.

Telecommunications systems use different tools to manage e-mail and to communicate on the Internet. These tools, often called **e-mail managers** or **mail readers,** may be built into the communications software you are using. Your e-mail manager will allow you to compose, read, print, save, and delete mail messages.

Netscape

If you are using Netscape Navigator, follow these steps to use your e-mail software:

1. Choose the e-mail option. You may have an envelope icon to click, or you may choose the *Netscape Mail* option in the **Window** menu.

Creating an E-Mail Message

2. Let's assume you want to send an e-mail message to one of your teachers about your study of e-mail and the Internet. Choose the option to create a new mail message. The message composition window will open. *Note:* You may have to type a password to have access to your e-mail software. If so, your teacher will tell you the password.

3. In the *To:* field, type the teacher's Internet address. Your teacher will provide the address to use.

4. Do not type anything in the *Cc:* field.
   Note: You would type an Internet address in this area only when you want to send a copy of your message to someone at the same time that you send the original message.

5. Move to the *Subject:* field, and type **Learning E-Mail.**
   Note: To move from one field to another, use the TAB key.

6. Do not type anything in the *Attachment:* field. You would type in this area only when you want to send files as attachments to a mail message.

Remember to follow the rules of netiquette.

7. Move to the message field, and type this message:

   [*Insert teacher's name*]**, you will be pleased to know that I am learning to use e-mail and the Internet. I'll soon be able to communicate with people all over the world. When I learn to use the Internet, I'll have many opportunities for hours of adventure, education, and fun.**

   [*Insert your name*]

8. Always proofread and edit your message to correct grammar, punctuation, and spelling errors.

9. Now that you have composed and edited your message, you are ready to send the message. Click on the Send button. You have now sent your e-mail message into cyberspace!

Reading an E-Mail Message

10. Whenever you want to read mail messages that were sent to you, choose the option to get mail or to view mail. After a brief pause, you will see a list of the files in your inbox.

11. Click a folder to display its messages. Choose the message *Welcome to the Internet!*
    Note: Your teacher should have sent you a *Welcome to the Internet!* e-mail message.

12. Read the entire message. Use the scroll bar and ARROW keys to view the other pages of the message.

13. As you read the message, think about whether you will want to print, save, download, or delete the message.

Printing an E-Mail Message

14. To print the message you have open on your screen, click on the Print button.

Saving an E-Mail Message

15. To save the message you have open on your screen to a new folder, choose the option to create a new folder. Type the name of the folder. You'll see the name of the new folder appear in the listing of folders in the message heading pane.

16. In the message heading pane, drag the name of the file to the newly created folder.
    Note: If you want to save a message to an existing folder, drag the name of the file to the name of that folder.

Working with an E-Mail Message

17. If you want to work with your e-mail message in your word processor, you must save the message as a text file. From the list of messages in your inbox, choose the message you want to download.

18. Choose *Save As* from the **File** menu, type the file name, and save the file as text to disk.
    Note: You can also copy a message and paste it into a word processing document.

Deleting an E-Mail Message

19. If you want to delete a message, highlight the message in the list of messages, and click on the Delete button.

Closing the E-Mail Software

20. To return to your browser, close the e-mail window.

Explorer

If you are using Microsoft Internet Explorer, follow these steps to use your e-mail software:

1. Click on the Mail button.

Creating an E-Mail Message

2. Let's assume you want to send an e-mail message to one of your teachers about your study of e-mail and the Internet. Choose the option to create a new mail message. The message composition window will open.

3. In the *To:* field, type the teacher's Internet address. Your teacher will provide the address to use.

4. Do not type anything in the *Cc:* field.
    Note: You would type an Internet address in this area only when you want to send a copy of your message to someone at the same time that you send the original message.

5. Move to the *Subject:* field, and type **Learning E-Mail**.
    Note: To move from one field to another, use the TAB key.

Remember to follow the rules of netiquette.

6. Move to the message field, and type this message:

   [*Insert teacher's name*], **you will be pleased to know that I am learning to use e-mail and the Internet. I'll soon be able to communicate with people all over the world. When I learn to use the Internet, I'll have many opportunities for hours of adventure, education, and fun.**

   [*Insert your name*]

7. Always proofread and edit your message to correct grammar, punctuation, and spelling errors.

8. Now that you have composed and edited your message, you are ready to send the message. Click on the Send button. You have now sent your e-mail message into cyberspace!

Reading an E-Mail Message

9. Whenever you want to read mail messages that were sent to you, choose the option to get mail or to read mail. After a brief pause, you will see a list of the messages (if any) in your inbox.
Note: You may have to click the Send and Receive button to download your mail.

10. Choose the message *Welcome to the Internet!*
Note: Your teacher should have sent you a *Welcome to the Internet!* e-mail message.

11. Read the entire message. Use the scroll bar and ARROW keys to view the other pages of the message.

12. As you read the message, think about whether you will want to print, save, download, or delete the message.

Printing an E-Mail Message

13. To print the message you have open on your screen, click on the Print button.

Saving an E-Mail Message

14. To save the message you have open on your screen, choose the *Save As* option from the **File** menu. Type a file name and save the file to disk.

Working with an E-Mail Message

15. If you want to work with your e-mail message in your word processor, you can copy/paste the message or save it to disk as a text file.

16. Choose *Save As* from the **File** menu, type the file name, and select the option to save as text.

Deleting an E-Mail Message

17. If you want to delete a message, highlight the message in the list of messages, and click on the Delete button.

Closing the E-Mail Software

18. To return to your browser, close the e-mail window.

Joining a Mailing List or Listserv

If you have a special interest, you might want to subscribe to a mailing list or listserv. A **listserv** is a discussion group focused on a particular interest area. Each listserv is composed of people who have voluntarily subscribed themselves. When one member of the listserv posts a message to the listserv, all members of the listserv will receive an e-mail message in their mailbox.

Therefore, if you subscribe to a list, check your mail regularly. Because subscribing to a mailing list can generate a lot of mail, you will soon get to know others who share interests similar to your own.

Important: There is no charge for joining a listserv. Just make sure you have your teacher's permission before you join a listserv.

Thousands of mailing lists exist on the Internet. To find a listserv that interests you, read books that provide lists of listservs by topic area, use a search engine and appropriate keywords, talk with others, or request a global list of listservs with an e-mail message.
Note: If you request a global list of listservs, use this address: **listserv@listserv.net** in your e-mail message. Your message should be as follows: **lists global/topic**. Insert the topic that interests you. When you receive the list, study it carefully to find the listservs that interest you.

Netscape

If you are using Netscape Navigator, follow these steps to join a listserv:

1. Select the e-mail option.

2. Because you must send an e-mail message to subscribe to a listserv, choose the option to create a new mail message.

3. In the *To:* field, type **listserv@** followed by the administrative address for the listserv.
   Note: The administrative address will be the second line of the resource listing.

   Important: Before you complete these steps, ask your teacher for permission to subscribe to a listserv and the name of the listserv.

4. Do not type anything in these fields: *Cc:*, *Subject:*, and *Attachment:*.
   Note: You may receive a prompt asking whether you want to include a subject. You do not want to include one.

5. Move to the message field, and type **subscribe** *listname your name*
   Note: Replace *listname* with the name of the listserv in which you are interested. Replace *your name* with your name.

6. Click on the Send button.

7. After a brief pause you will receive a confirmation request from the listserv. Use the reply feature of your e-mail software, and type this message: **OK**. You have now subscribed to a listserv.
   Note: Remember to check your e-mail frequently. You may receive lots of mail.

8. If you want to unsubscribe to a listserv, repeat steps 1 through 6 except type this message: **unsubscribe** *listname*
   Note: Replace *listname* with the name of the listserv. Your address will be removed from the listserv.

Explorer

If you are using Microsoft Internet Explorer, follow these steps to join a listserv:

1. Select the e-mail option.

2. Because you must send an e-mail message to subscribe to a listserv, choose the option to create a new mail message.

3. In the *To:* field, type **listserv@** followed by the administrative address for the listserv.
   Note: The administrative address will be the second line of the resource listing.

   Important: Before you complete these steps, ask your teacher for permission to subscribe to a listserv and the name of the listserv.

4. Do not type anything in these fields: *Cc* or *Subject.*
   Note: You may receive a prompt asking whether you want to include a subject. You do not want to include one.

5. Move to the message field, and type **subscribe** *listname your name*
   Note: Replace *listname* with the name of the listserv in which you are interested. Replace *your name* with your name.

6. Click on the Send button.

7. After a brief pause you will receive a confirmation request from the listserv. Use the reply feature of your e-mail software, and type this message: **OK.** You have now subscribed to a listserv.
   Note: Remember to check your e-mail frequently. You may receive lots of mail.

8. If you want to unsubscribe to a listserv, repeat steps 1 through 6 except type this message: **unsubscribe** *listname*
   Note: Replace *listname* with the name of the listserv. Your address will be removed from the listserv.

Accessing News and Conference Areas

The newsgroups to which you have access may depend on the service your ISP provides. Your teacher will tell you whether you have access to newsgroups.

Just like the newspaper that you may have delivered to your doorstep, news is delivered to your computer on a monthly, daily, hourly, and minute-by-minute basis on the Internet. Most news services update articles (or postings) as the news happens, and they organize the articles by topic. **Newsgroups** or **conferences** provide areas for you to exchange ideas, ask questions, offer opinions, or just do some **lurking** (reading without expressing an opinion to the group). Most news and conference areas are organized according to related topics. You can choose a topic to investigate and read specific news articles. If you want to communicate with others on the topic, you can reply to an article.

Netscape

If you are using Netscape Navigator, follow these steps to access a newsgroup:

Important: As you explore newsgroups, always remember to leave an objectionable site quickly by clicking the Home button. You will immediately return to the home page set up for your browser.

1. If you know the name of the newsgroup you want to access, type **news:** followed by the name in the Location box of the browser, and skip to step 6. For example, type **news:biz.general** and press ENTER/RETURN.

Newsgroup articles are plain text with limited links.

2. To find a newsgroup, choose *Netscape News* from the **Window** menu. To view the list of newsgroups offered by your ISP, open the news folder, and choose *Show All Newsgroups* from the **Options** menu. An

alphabetical list of newsgroups will appear. This process may take a few minutes the first time the newsgroup list is downloaded to your computer.

3. Scroll down to the *biz.** folder. This newsgroup is dedicated to business topics.

4. Open the folder to display a list of the various newsgroups.

5. Select the *biz.general* newsgroup. After a few moments a list of articles will appear.
   Note: You may use the Find option on the **File** menu to search for specific text in articles.

6. Choose an article that interests you.

7. Read the article when it appears on your screen.

8. After you read the article, you can mail, save, download, print, or react to the article. Access online help for the steps to perform these actions.
   Note: If you reply to the article, remember that everyone in the newsgroup will read your reply.

9. When you are finished reading articles from the newsgroup, close the newsgroup window.

Explorer

If you are using Microsoft Internet Explorer, follow these steps to access a newsgroup:

Important: As you explore newsgroups, always remember to leave an objectionable site quickly by clicking the Home button. You will immediately return to the home page set up for your browser.

1. If you know the name of the newsgroup you want to access, type **news:** followed by the name in the Address box of the browser, and skip to step 5. For example, type **news:biz.general** and press ENTER/RETURN.

2. To find a newsgroup, click the Mail button and choose *Read News.* To view the list of newsgroups offered by your ISP, click the *Newsgroups* button. An alphabetical list of newsgroups will appear. This process may take a few minutes the first time the newsgroup list is downloaded to your computer.

3. Type **biz** in the *Display newsgroups which contain:* field, and then scroll to the *biz.general* newsgroup. This newsgroup is dedicated to business topics.

4. Select the *biz.general* newsgroup, and click the Go to button. After a few moments a list of articles will appear.
   Note: Do not subscribe to any newsgroups if the program prompts you to do so.

5. Choose an article that interests you.

6. Read the article when it appears on your screen.

7. After you read the article, you can mail, save, download, print, or react to the article. Access online help for the steps to perform these actions.
   Note: If you reply to the article, remember that everyone in the newsgroup will read your reply.

Newsgroup articles are plain text with limited links.

8. When you are finished reading articles from the newsgroup, close the newsgroup window.

Exiting Your Computer Session

Just as you will learn how to surf the Net on a routine basis, you will quickly learn how to quit your session at the computer.

Netscape

If you are using Netscape Navigator, follow these steps to end your computer session:

1. Click on the **File** menu.

2. Choose *Exit* (Windows) or *Quit* (Macintosh).

Explorer

If you are using Microsoft Internet Explorer, follow these steps to end your computer session:

1. Click on the **File** menu.

2. Choose *Exit* (Windows) or *Quit* (Macintosh).

▶ **Part**

One Two Three

123

Activities

Activity 1
Surfin' the Net

Now that you are somewhat familiar with basic Internet terms, how to launch your browser, and how to access information on the Internet, are you ready to jump in and surf the Net? Are you ready for adventure after adventure as you explore the Internet and the new world of information at your fingertips?

As you complete each activity in this book, you will learn something about the Internet, the World Wide Web, your browser, or the topic of research. In many instances you will explore on your own as you surf, but you will also learn from your classmates and teacher when you share about your adventures and experiences through written and oral communication.

Activity 1 provides an opportunity to work with a team to review the material in the Introduction. As you and your team work together, remember to learn from each other so you will be comfortable when you surf on your own beginning in Activity 2.

After you complete this activity, you will be able to:

- Launch your browser.
- Identify and explore the basic features of your browser.
- Access online help.
- Surf on your own.
- Exit your browser.

To increase your confidence level in surfing the Net, let's explore with a team.

Your browser allows you to access information on the Internet.

1. With your assigned team members, launch your browser. A blank page or the home page setup for your browser should appear on your screen. If you are using Netscape Navigator, you may see a screen similar to Figure 2-1 on page 26. If you are using Microsoft Internet Explorer, you may see a screen similar to Figure 2-2 on page 26.
   Note: Remember, you may review the steps to launch your browser in the Introduction.

2. Now what? Take time to carefully review the features of your browser.
   Note: Review the material in the Introduction, as needed.
   ▶ Identify the basic features of your browser.
   ▶ Identify the directory buttons.
   ▶ Identify the menus.

Sometimes you may have to scroll through information to see the entire page and the hypertext links.

3. To review the types of information you will see each time you launch your browser, scroll down the home page. If your browser starts with a blank page, skip to step 4.
   ▶ What is the URL for the home page of your browser?
   ▶ Can you identify the links on the home page of your browser?

Figure 2-1
Netscape Navigator Home
Page

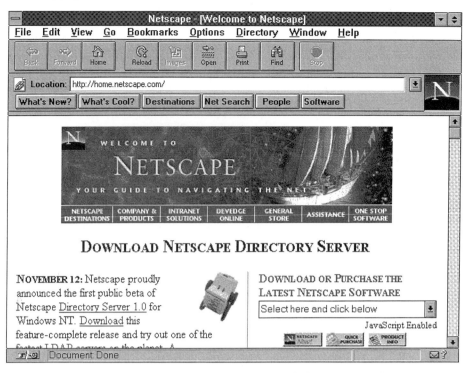

Figure 2-2
Microsoft Internet Explorer
Home Page

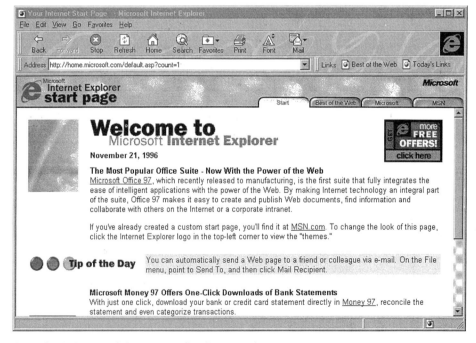

Note: Keep your journal nearby as you surf the Net. Get into the habit of recording information you may want to refer to later.

4. To review the types of helpful information available from your browser, access online help. Review the categories of information, and explore the options.
Note: Learn to access online help before you ask others for help.

5. By now you have probably learned that changes occur all the time on the Internet. Some sites may be here today and gone tomorrow, and new sites appear every day. Explore your browser features to learn what sites are new. Scroll down the list of new sites.

   ▶ What feature from your browser provides a listing of new sites?
   ▶ Identify three new sites that interest you.

You are personally responsible for respecting the school's acceptable use policy. Net surfing requires self-discipline.

6. As you link from one page to another in your surfing adventures, always remember that you can back out of a site easily and you have a fast way home if you feel like you are lost or outside of your comfort zone. You are required to remember the acceptable use policy at all times when you surf the Net.
Note: Instead of going back through several pages, use your browser to "go" directly to a previously viewed page. If you are using a text browser, refer to the navigation commands to go back a page.

   ▶ How do you back out of a site?
   ▶ How do you return immediately to the home page of your browser?

7. When you know the URL for a site, you may type the address in the site location or address field. Go directly to the Excite home page at this URL: **http://www.excite.com/**

   ▶ Did the Excite home page appear on your screen?

8. Go quickly to the home page for your browser.
Note: Remember, you may use one of the features of your browser.

9. Some browsers offer a bookmark feature to identify a list of favorite sites that are interesting, humorous, or helpful. Brief descriptions of each of the listed sites provide an overview of the site. Explore your browser features to identify these sites.

   ▶ What feature from your browser identifies these sites?
   ▶ Identify three sites that appeal to you.

10. Exit your browser.

11. In a team discussion, evaluate the ability of each person to launch your browser, use the navigation tools, access online help, and exit your browser. Discuss how you may use the Internet in your school and home activities.

Activity 2
Getting World Facts

Get into the habit of adding a bookmark or favorite page whenever you access a page you want to revisit.

Have you ever prepared a research paper? Did you spend hours in the library searching for related information in books or journals or on videos or CD-ROMs? You can save lots of time by using the Internet as a research tool. As you explore different sites and pages, also get into the habit of determining whether a particular page would be useful in the future.

A popular and useful web site is that of the Central Intelligence Agency (CIA). This site offers background information about the CIA, publications, community links, and other useful research information. By linking to the CIA's World Factbook publication, you can access facts about countries all over the world, including their geography, people, government, economy, transportation, communications, and defense forces. If you want to analyze different regions of the world, you may research facts for comparison data and then evaluate your findings.

After you complete this activity, you will be able to:

- Locate data about a specific country on the Internet.
- Conduct research on telephone systems throughout the world.
- Use the Find or Search command from your browser.
- Compose a report about your research.

To learn about telephone systems in the world, let's explore the Internet.

1. Launch your browser to begin your exploration.

You may access online help whenever you want.

2. Go to the Central Intelligence Agency web site at this URL:
    http://www.odci.gov/cia/
    Note: Read the information on this page, and link to the next page. Scroll through the information to see the entire page and the hypertext links.

Remember to type the URL exactly as shown.

3. Link to Publications and then to The World Factbook. Your screen should be similar to the Central Intelligence Agency's The World Factbook page in Figure 2-3 on page 29.

Your screen may vary from Figure 2-3 if the CIA made changes to the page since the publication of this book.

4. Locate and scroll through the information about the United States. *Note:* The countries are arranged alphabetically. Link to U and then to United States.

Access online help for the steps to use the Find or Search command.

5. To research information about the telephone system in the United States, go to the beginning of the information on the United States. Then, using the Find or Search command from your browser, type **telephone** and process the request. Your browser will immediately display information about the telephone system in the United States. *Note:* When you access online help, link to the specific information you need to review to be able to complete a task.

Figure 2-3
Central Intelligence
Agency's The World
Factbook Page

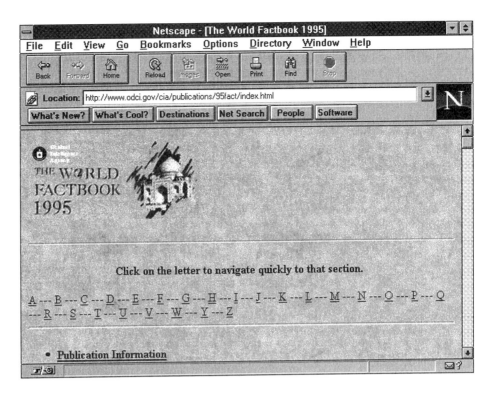

6. On a separate sheet of paper, record the following information:
   ▶ the types and number of telephones available
   ▶ the local data
   ▶ the intercity information
   ▶ the international data

7. Go back to the listing of the countries and research the telephone system data for two other countries.
   Note: Remember to record the information for these countries.

8. Exit your browser.

9. Using your word processing or desktop publishing software, compose a one-page report with conclusions about your research.
   Note: If you want to copy or paraphrase information that appeared on a web page in a report you are creating, you must include a citation to identify the source reference or origin of the material—just as you would do for information you copy or paraphrase from a printed source.
   ▶ What did you learn about the telephone system in the countries you explored?
   ▶ Which country is more advanced in their use of telephone systems?
   ▶ Which country has only minimal telephone service?
   ▶ What conclusions can you make from your research?
   ▶ Identify how you will be able to use the Central Intelligence Agency web site in your personal, school, or work activities.

Be a responsible writer, and always give credit to others for their ideas and information.

Activity 3
Visiting the United States Postal Service

Have you ever had to stand in line to buy stamps at the post office? Have you ever called the post office for a ZIP code to complete a mailing address? With access to the Internet, you no longer need to stand in line to buy stamps or spend time on the phone waiting for information. Postal information is available on the Internet seven days a week, twenty-four hours a day—and with no lines.

When you explore the United States Postal Service site on the Internet, you will find many options that save time and improve your productivity. At the United States Postal Service site, you can see what the newest stamps look like (if you're using a graphical browser), learn the history of the stamps, and learn how to order stamps. You can find a ZIP code without having to call the post office. And you can access information about mailing options, formatting addresses for faster delivery of your mail, and packaging material you want to mail.

After you complete this activity, you will be able to:

- Find the ZIP code for a specific street address in any city in the United States.
- Find which city is associated with a specific ZIP code.
- Use acceptable postal abbreviations.
- Use correct formatting for envelopes.
- Identify a new stamp and its history.
- Identify the differences between mailing options.
- Use your browser to add a bookmark.
- Compose a memorandum.

To learn about the United States Postal Service, let's explore the Internet.

1. Launch your browser to begin your exploration of United States Postal Service (USPS).

2. Go to the United States Postal Service web site at this URL: **http://www.usps.gov/**

If your browser seems to take too long to go to a site, verify that you typed the correct URL.

3. Link to Your Post Office. Notice the hypertext links on the Your Post Office page.
   Note: Remember the contents and links on a web page may change at any time. When you explore a page looking for information, try to find links that match your search criteria.

4. To find ZIP codes, link to ZIP Codes. Then link to the ZIP+4 Code Lookup page.

Realize that information that travels across the Internet is not confidential; anyone can "grab" your name and address.

5. In the appropriate fields, type your name, city, and state, and process the ZIP code request.
   ▶ What ZIP code did the USPS provide for your address?

6. Perform several ZIP code requests.
   ▶ What is the ZIP code for your school?
   ▶ What is the ZIP code for this address: 7155 High Sierra Circle, West Palm Beach, Florida?
   ▶ What is the ZIP code for Procter & Gamble Co., 630 Main Street, Cincinnati, Ohio?

7. Suppose you have a ZIP code but do not know the city and state associated with the ZIP or you want to know the ZIP code for a particular city. To secure such information easily, go back to the ZIP Code Lookup and Address Information page. Link to City State/ZIP Code Associations.
   ▶ What city has the ZIP code 38912?
   ▶ What are the ZIP codes for Murfreesboro, Tennessee?

Scroll through the information to see the entire page and the hypertext links.

8. Go back to the Your Post Office page, and link to Addressing. Scroll down through the page to read about acceptable abbreviations, guidelines for addressing mail, and packaging and addressing parcels.
   ▶ What is the state abbreviation for the state in which you live?
   ▶ What is the standard postal abbreviation for the word *boulevard*?
   ▶ How can you save an addressee a trip to the post office to pick up a parcel?

Use your browser to "go" directly to a previously viewed page.

9. Go back to the Your Post Office page, and link to Stamps. Then link to What's New in Stamps, Stamps Information, and Order Information to answer these questions.
   ▶ Identify a new stamp.
   ▶ What does the new stamp look like?
   Note: To see the image of a new stamp, first link to the news about the stamp. Then link to the name of the stamp in the title of the article. (If you are using a text browser, you won't be able to see the stamp image.)
   ▶ How do you order stamps?

10. At the Your Post Office page, explore the Consumer Information to learn about mailing tips.
    ▶ How do you retrieve a letter you have already mailed?
    ▶ What is the difference between priority mail and express mail?

11. Using your browser, add a bookmark for the Your Post Office page.
    Note: If you are using Netscape Navigator, choose Bookmark to mark a page. (See Figure 2-4 on page 32.) If you are using Microsoft Internet Explorer, choose Favorites to mark a page. (See Figure 2-5 on page 32.) If you are using a text browser, access online help for the directions to add a bookmark.

12. Exit your browser.

Figure 2-4
Bookmark Menu from
Netscape Navigator
Browser

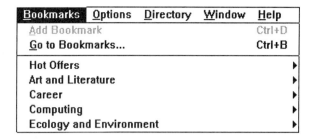

Figure 2-5
Favorites Menu from
Microsoft Internet Explorer
Browser

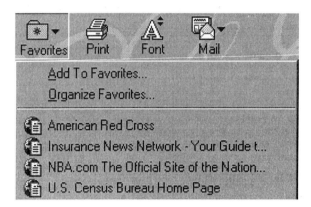

13. Using your word processing software, compose a memorandum to your teacher.

   ▸ Describe how you were impressed with the information on the Your Post Office pages.

   ▸ Identify how you will use the United States Postal Service site for personal, work, or school activities.

Activity 4
Observing the Weather

All you have to do is look outside to see whether it is sunny or rainy. And you can guess the approximate temperature when you step outside. But do you know what the actual temperature is in your area? Do you know whether rain or snow is forecasted for today? Is your town experiencing a particular weather pattern? Would you like to know what the weather is like in a coastal city of the United States or in another country?

Just because you didn't hear the weather forecast on the morning or evening news doesn't mean you have to wait until the next weather report on the radio or television. You can learn what the weather is by accessing The Weather Channel on the Internet. You'll then know exactly what clothes to wear today and what plans to make for the evening. You can also study weather conditions in different parts of the world to help you understand the seasons.

After you complete this activity, you will be able to:

- Find current and forecasted weather for cities in the United States and in the world.
- Learn about storms.
- Increase your weather vocabulary.
- Use your browser to mark a favorite page.
- Compose a memo.

To learn about The Weather Channel, let's explore the Internet.

1. Launch your browser to begin your exploration of The Weather Channel.

2. Go to The Weather Channel web site at this URL:
   http://www.weather.com/
   Your screen should be similar to The Weather Channel home page in Figure 2-6 on page 34. Notice the types of information available at this site.

   The top-level domain com identifies The Weather Channel site as a commercial service web site.

3. Link to <u>The Weather</u>, and request the weather for your state and city (or nearby city).
   - What is the weather forecast for today?
   - What is the current temperature?
   - What is the weather forecast for tomorrow?
   - When was the weather last updated?

4. So that you may access the local weather quickly in the future, add a bookmark for this page.

   Access online help to review how to add a bookmark or mark a favorite page.

5. Carefully review the weather forecast for this week. On a separate sheet of paper, record any weather terms you don't understand, such as *relative humidity* and *Doppler radar*.

Figure 2-6
The Weather Channel
Home Page

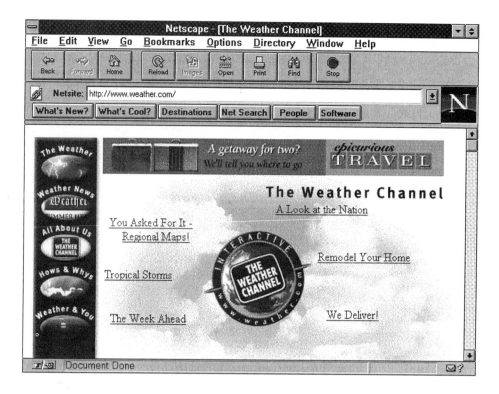

6. Locate and record the definitions of the weather terms you didn't understand.
   Note: First link to <u>Hows and Whys</u>, then to the <u>Teacher's Resources</u> and the <u>Weather Glossary</u>.

7. Add a bookmark for this page.

Use your browser to "go" directly to a previously viewed page.

8. Go back to the Teacher's Resources page, and link to the information on heat index and windchill.

   ▶ What two factors affect the heat index?
   ▶ What is the windchill temperature if the actual temperature outside is 20 degrees Fahrenheit and the wind is blowing at 10 miles per hour?

9. Go back to the Teacher's Resources page, and link to the information on storms. Read about hurricanes.

   ▶ What pattern exists in the names of tropical storms?

10. Go back to the Tropical Storms & Hurricanes page, and link to the information on <u>Storm Names</u>. Read about retired storm names.

    ▶ Have you ever heard about any of the storms whose names are retired?

The content and links on a web page may change at any time. Explore the page to find links that match your search criteria.

11. Go back to The Weather Channel home page, and explore the weather in another country. Choose a country link (other than your own country) and then a city link.
    Note: Link first to <u>Weather</u> and then to <u>International Conditions and Forecasts</u>.

    ▶ In what city and country did you choose to explore the weather?

> ▸ How do the temperatures compare with the weather you are experiencing in your area?
>
> ▸ To what do you attribute the differences?

12. Explore the weather conditions in several parts of the world that you want to visit someday.
Note: Because you can check the weather anywhere in the world, you may want to add a bookmark for this page.

13. Exit your browser.

14. Using your word processing software, compose a memo to your teacher.

> ▸ Summarize what you learned at The Weather Channel site.
>
> ▸ Identify at least two instances in which you or your school may use The Weather Channel.

Activity 5
Improving Your Writing and Speaking Skills

Businesses are highly dependent on employees who possess the ability to communicate effectively. Effective communication skills help employers and colleagues make decisions, manage operations, and plan for the future. Your communication skills will also determine the first impression you make on others.

How would you evaluate your communication skills? Do you write and speak with confidence? Do you apply these characteristics of effective communication to all your writing and speaking situations: conciseness, clarity, completeness, correctness, and concreteness?

Learning to write and to speak effectively is hard work, and often you must study material you have heard about since your elementary school days. If you will take time to assess your communication skills honestly and then address your weaknesses related to writing and speaking skills, you will undoubtedly improve your chances for success in your school, work, and personal activities.

After you complete this activity, you will be able to:

- Access an online writing lab, and review the basics of writing.
- Apply the characteristics of effective communication in written and oral situations.
- Compose a memo.

To develop your communication skills, let's explore the Internet.

1. Launch your browser to begin your exploration.

The top-level domain *edu* identifies The Purdue University On-line Writing Lab web site as an education site.

2. Go to The Purdue University On-line Writing Lab (OWL) home page at this URL: **http://owl.trc.purdue.edu/**
   Note the links on this page.

3. Link to <u>Resources for Writing</u>, and then link to <u>outline</u>. Your screen should be similar to the Owl Handouts: An Outline of all the Documents page in Figure 2-7 on page 37. Scroll the entire page to review the links.

4. Scroll to the section on Sentence Concerns. Explore the information on Common Errors.
   - What is the difference between a run-on sentence and a comma splice?
   - What is a fused sentence?

Use your browser to "go" directly to a previously viewed page.

5. Go back to Sentence Concerns, and explore the information on Sentence Punctuation.
   - How many types of sentence patterns are there?
   - When do you use a semicolon?

Figure 2-7
Owl Handouts Page

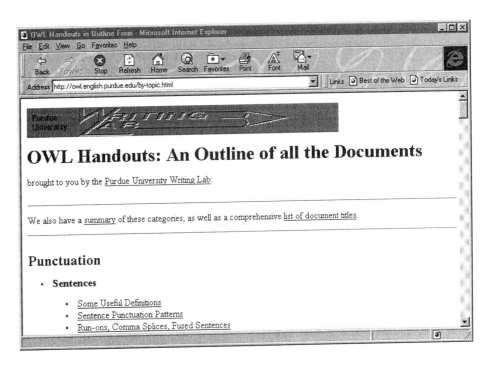

6. Go back to Sentence Concerns, and continue exploring these links: <u>Dangling Modifiers</u>, <u>Fragments</u>, <u>Parallel Structure</u>, <u>Definitions</u>, and <u>Active/Passive Voice in Verbs</u>.
   - ▸ What are the characteristics of a dangling modifier?
   - ▸ How can you revise sentences to avoid dangling modifiers?
   - ▸ What is another name for an incomplete sentence?
   - ▸ What is an independent clause?
   - ▸ What is the difference between active and passive voice?

7. Assess your strengths and weaknesses related to written communication.
   - ▸ In what areas do you feel comfortable?
   - ▸ In what areas do you think you need help?
   - ▸ How are your grammar and punctuation skills?

8. Go back to the Owl Handouts page, and explore appropriate links to address the weaknesses that you identified in step 7.
   Note: Some areas have practice exercises that you can complete if your time allows.

Remember you can use the Find or Search command to locate a word or phrase on a page.

9. Go back to the Owl Handouts page, and link to <u>Writing Report Abstracts</u> in the Business/Professional Writing section.
   - ▸ Identify two types of abstracts.
   - ▸ Identify two qualities of a good abstract.

10. From the Owl Handouts page, link to <u>Adding Emphasis</u>.
    - ▸ Which punctuation marks have more emphatic force?
    - ▸ Which positions in a sentence are more emphatic?

11. From the Owl Handouts page, explore the information in these links: <u>Revision in Business Writing</u>, <u>Business Letters: Subordinating</u>

Negatives in Good News and Neutral Messages, Sales Letters: Four Point Action Closing, Psychological Detail and Dramatization, and Memo Writing.

- ▶ Why should you revise a document?
- ▶ How can you subordinate a negative idea in a message?
- ▶ What are the four points for a strong action closing in a sales message?
- ▶ What is *dramatization*?
- ▶ Identify the basic parts of a memo.

12. Exit your browser.

13. Using your word processing software, compose a memo to your teacher outlining what you have learned in this activity and how you will use The Purdue University On-line Writing Lab site for your school, home, and work communication activities.

14. Review the written documents you prepared for Activities 2, 3, and 4. Revise the documents to apply what you have learned in this activity. Explore related links at The Purdue University On-line Writing Lab site if you need additional information in the revision process.

Activity 6
Analyzing the United States Department of State

Do you understand global market information?

With technological advancements and numerous transportation options in the world today, many companies conduct business in more than one country. As a result of international business, consumers have more choices for products and services. Workers have increased career opportunities. And to be successful, international businesses must communicate effectively. Because of the expanding business world, your study of the Internet is even more critical to prepare you for the global marketplace when you graduate.

To be a team player and to contribute to the success of a business, you should understand the importance of business, how to work with people, and the competition factor in the foreign economic policy of the United States. Government documents on the Internet will help you learn this information and plan for the future—especially if you work for an international company.

Where can you find government documents related to foreign policy? The United States Department of State is the leading United States foreign affairs agency. This agency is responsible for implementing the president's foreign policies. The web site for this agency includes links to valuable information related to the global market.

After you complete this activity, you will be able to:

- Identify the importance of a global marketplace.
- Identify facts about a foreign country.
- Locate travel warnings for specific foreign countries.
- Print or save an article to disk.
- Compose a written report.

To learn about the United States Department of State, let's explore the Internet.

1. Launch your browser to begin your exploration of the U.S. Department of State web site.

The top-level domain gov identifies the U.S. Department of State site as a government web site.

2. With your assigned team members, go to the U.S. Department of State web site at this URL: **http://www.state.gov/**
   Your screen should be similar to the U.S. Department of State home page in Figure 2-8 on page 40. Notice the various categories of information on the home page.

3. Choose several links to scan articles, and find an article related to United States foreign policy.
   Note: You may want to link first with the <u>Hot Topics</u> category.

4. Scan the article to determine whether the article interests you. Locate another article, if necessary. You may want to save, print, or copy and

Figure 2-8
U.S. Department of State
Home Page

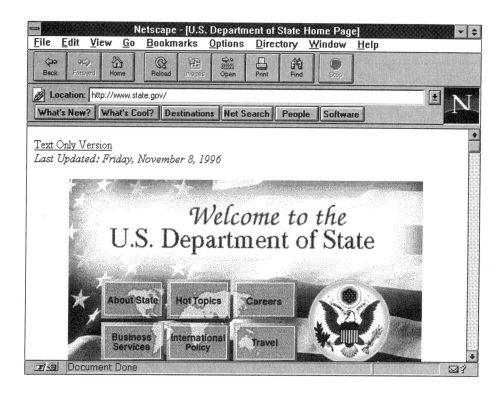

paste the information you locate to help your team prepare a report at the end of this activity.

Note: Ask your teacher whether you should save information to disk, print the information, or copy and paste the information.

5. Go back to the U.S. Department of State home page, and link to <u>Travel</u>. Research travel warnings for a specific country.

6. Exit your browser. Read the article you saved, printed, or copied.
Note: If you saved a file to disk or copied a file, you will need to open the file from your word processing software.

7. Using your word processing or desktop publishing software, compose a one-page report to your social studies or history teacher.
Note: If you want to copy or paraphrase information that appeared on a web page in your report, you must provide a citation to identify the source reference or origin of the material.

   ▸ Include a brief summary of the article you read.
   ▸ What conclusions can you make from the article?
   ▸ What conclusions can you make about the travel warnings for the country you researched?
   ▸ Identify several ways that the U.S. Department of State web site will be useful to you in your future study of foreign affairs.

Activity 7
Exploring National Parks

Have you ever been to a national park? If you have, what can you remember about the park? Did you have a back-to-nature experience by camping in a tent, cooking over a campfire, and surviving the weather? Did you hike through the woods identifying different trees and plants? Did you see any wildlife in the park? Were you impressed with the beauty of nature and the excitement of a new learning experience?

The national park system is one of our most precious resources in the United States. Nearly every state has parks and monuments that people visit to escape from their hectic worlds and to learn about nature, the environment, history, geography, ecology, and wildlife. Are you familiar with the national parks in your geographical area?

With the Internet you can explore the world of outdoor recreation and national history from various World Wide Web sites. Because you can see pictures from the parks, hiking trails, and accommodations (if you have a graphical browser) and review lists of special events, your exploration can help you and your family determine where you want to travel. You can also gather historical facts and geographical data for research purposes.

After you complete this activity, you will be able to:

- Research a national park of interest to you.
- Print a page with information about the park.
- Send an e-mail message.
- Use a search engine to explore for additional park information.
- Prepare notes and a visual aid for an informative oral report.

To learn about national parks, let's explore the Internet.

1. Launch your browser to begin your exploration of national parks.

2. Go to The National Park Service ParkNet home page at this URL: **http://www.nps.gov/**

The top-level domain gov identifies The National Park Service ParkNet site as a government web site.

3. As shown in Figure 2-9 on page 42, The National Park Service ParkNet home page allows you to explore information about national parks. Link to <u>Visit Your Parks</u> to begin your search for a national park.

Learn all you can about a national park by exploring link after link.

4. Explore the various links on the Visit Your National Parks page to choose a park to research. Then browse to learn all you can about this park.
   Note: You may want to save, print, or copy and paste the information you locate to help you prepare for your oral report at the end of this activity. Access online help to learn how to save to disk an image that appears on a web page. You may include the image in your presentation.
   ▸ What is the name of the national park?
   ▸ Where is the park located?

Figure 2-9
The National Park Service
ParkNet Home Page

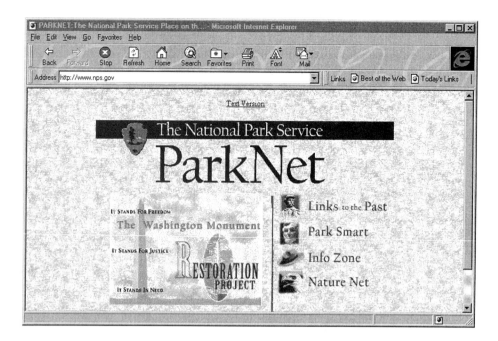

- ▶ What are the directions to the park?
- ▶ What accommodations are available, and how do you make reservations?
- ▶ What are the operating hours and seasons?
- ▶ What special events are on their calendar?
- ▶ What is the phone number, mailing address, and e-mail address for the park?

5. *Optional:* If additional information is available by e-mail communication, send an e-mail message to the national park.
   Note: Remember to include a subject in all e-mail messages.

Review basic netiquette guidelines in the Introduction.

6. Does any other information exist on the Internet about the park you chose? Let's use the search engine, AltaVista, to explore for additional park information on the Internet. Go to the AltaVista web site at this URL: **http://www.altavista.digital.com/**
   Note: Here are the URLs for other popular search engines:

A search engine will allow you to search on the Internet for information on a particular topic.

Lycos	**http://www.lycos.com/**
Yahoo	**http://www.yahoo.com/**
Excite	**http://www.excite.com/**
Magellan	**http://www.mckinley.com/**

7. Scroll down the page to move to the field where you can enter the words you want the search engine to look for. Type the park name, and process the search request.
   Note: Within seconds you should see a list of the sites and pages that include a reference to the park. Review the results of the search, and read a posting that interests you.

   - ▶ How successful was your search?
   - ▶ Did your search link you to The National Park Service site?
   - ▶ How might you use a search engine for school activities?

Remember, always provide a source reference to give credit to others for their work.

8. When you find a posting that interests you, decide whether you want to save, print, or copy and paste the information you locate to help you prepare your report in this activity.

9. Exit your browser.

10. Using your word processing or desktop publishing software and your presentation software, prepare notes and a visual aid for an informative oral report about the national park you researched. Identify how the national park sites will be helpful to your family and to your school.

Activity 8
Desperately Seeking Someone

Have you ever had a close friend or relative move to another part of town or to another city or state and leave no forwarding address? Or perhaps you or your parents lost the address of a friend or relative. Before now, when you wanted to communicate with that person, you had no way to do so. Could the Internet help you locate an address for someone?

Through the use of a search engine from your browser, you may be able to find information about an individual—at no cost except the value of your time. You can sometimes find addresses, telephone numbers, and e-mail addresses. Should you someday want to find similar information about a business, you can also search the Internet.

After you complete this activity, you will be able to:

- Use a search engine to locate information for an individual on the Internet.
- View and print address maps.
- Find points of interest for a geographical location.
- Orally discuss your findings.
- Compose a personal letter.

> Examples of popular search engines for finding people and companies include Lycos, Yahoo, Infoseek, Magellan, Excite, and Switchboard.

To learn about finding information about someone, let's explore the Internet.

1. Before you begin working on the Internet, identify someone (a friend or relative) you want to locate.
   Note: You may want to talk with your family or friends to identify the name of an individual to locate on the Internet.

2. Launch your browser to begin your exploration.

3. Let's use the search engine, Lycos, to help us find information on the Internet. Go to the Lycos web site at this URL:
   http://www.lycos.com/

4. Do you know whether *your* name, address, and phone number are listed on the Internet? Scroll down the Lycos home page and link to <u>People Find</u>. Your screen should be similar to the PeopleFind page in Figure 2-10 on page 45.
   Note: In most cases individuals are listed on the Internet if they have a listed phone number. If someone has an unlisted phone number, you won't be able to access information. Consider under whose name the phone may be listed. For instance, if you live with your parents, your home phone may be listed under one or both of your parents' names, but not your name.

5. Move to the fields where you can enter known information about an individual. Type your last name, first name, city, and state. Then process the search request.

> A search engine will allow you to search on the Internet for information on a particular topic.

Figure 2-10
Lycos PeopleFind Page
with Input Fields

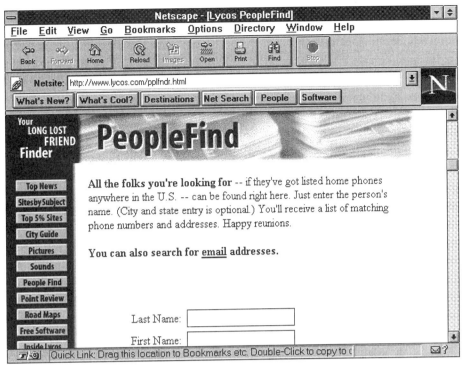

Note: The results of your search will vary. (1) You may receive exactly one match. (2) If you receive more than one match, you must scroll through the results to determine whether any of the results truly match your request. In some cases you may have to make phone calls or send e-mail messages to determine whether you have actually found your friend or relative. (3) If no matches occur with the given search, first verify the accuracy of the information you entered. You may also need to reconsider whether the individual's phone number may be listed under a different name.

▶ Did you find a listing for your home?
▶ Is your address correct?
▶ Is your phone number correct?

Use your browser to "go" directly to a previously viewed page.

6. Go back to the PeopleFind page. To search for information about a relative or friend, type all the known information in the appropriate fields. Then process the search request.
Note: If you do not know the information for a particular field, leave the field empty.

▶ Did you find a listing for your relative or friend?
▶ What is the person's address?

Using a given address, you may access links to maps and businesses.

7. Let's assume you do not know exactly where this address is located. Link to the person's address, and then link to maps and businesses in the neighborhood. Then explore the links to view the location on a map if you have a graphical browser, to locate specific businesses, and to find specific information about the town.

- ▶ The address is located near what major city?
- ▶ What is the name of the nearest major road?
- ▶ How many elementary schools are located within five miles of this address?
- ▶ What is the address for a nearby post office?
- ▶ How many Italian restaurants are located within ten miles of this address?

8. *Optional:* Ask your teacher if you may print a map (if you have a graphical browser).
   - ▶ What options affect the degree of detail in a map?
   - ▶ Identify instances when you might want to print a map for school, home, or work activities.

9. Exit your browser.

10. In an assigned team, discuss your experience using a search engine.
    - ▶ Were you successful in your searches?
    - ▶ If you were unsuccessful in finding the information, brainstorm about why you might not have been able to find the information.
    - ▶ Brainstorm about the ways you may use search engines to locate people.
    - ▶ Does the PeopleFind feature violate rights to privacy?
    - ▶ Discuss the instances in which you might use the maps.

11. Using your word processing software, compose a personal letter to the individual you located on the Internet. Be sure to explain how you found the person's address.

Activity 9
Helping Your School

Take a minute to think about your school, its clubs and organizations, its awards and scholarships, and the student activities. Would you like to make a major contribution to your school? Are you active in any of your school clubs or organizations? Do you know whether a group at your school needs help with projects and activities? Could your school benefit in some way if you communicated with students and teachers at other high schools across the nation?

You may be able to answer these questions by visiting a web site where you can participate actively in student activities across the nation. The National Association of Secondary Schools Principals (also known as NASSP) is the nation's largest school leadership organization. The NASSP web site offers information not only about NASSP and its services but also about student activities across the nation. At this site student councils across the nation post projects or student activities that others may use or adapt to help schools educate students more effectively.

After you complete this activity, you will be able to:

- Identify school projects and activities.
- Select a school project or activity to consider for your school.
- Compose and distribute a survey.
- Analyze the survey results and make a recommendation to your school.
- Be a leader for your school.

To learn about student activities that allow you to make a contribution to your school, let's explore the Internet.

1. Begin your exploration by launching your browser.

2. With your assigned team members, go to the National Association of Secondary Schools Principals (NASSP) web site at this URL:
   http://www.nassp.org/
   Note: View the links on this home page.

The top-level domain org identifies the NASSP site as an organization web site.

3. Link to <u>What's New</u> to learn what students and leaders have accomplished or plan to do. Read about the accomplishments or plans that interest you.

4. Go back to the NASSP home page, and link to <u>Student Activities</u>. The Student Activities page, as shown in Figure 2-11 on page 48, identifies student groups that sponsor activities across the nation. Scroll down the page to read the listings for projects and activities that might interest you and others at your school.

5. Explore the links to the postings of student activities that appeal to your group. As a team, decide upon one student activity or project to pursue for your school.

Figure 2-11
Student Activities Page

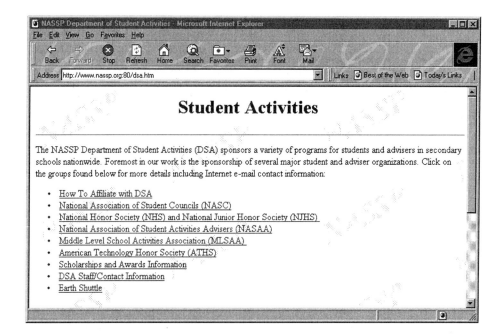

Note: You may want to print descriptive pages of the selected student activity or project so you will have information to share with your teacher and others.

6. Exit your browser.

7. Discuss your team's decision with your teacher and establish a communication plan.
   Note: Secure your teacher's approval for your project selection before you proceed with this activity. You may also need to talk with a school administrator to verify that your selected project is appropriate for your school. Be sure to discuss with whom you should communicate; consider classmates, teachers, parents, and administrators.

Carefully edit and proofread your survey *before* you distribute it.

8. Using your word processing software, compose a one-page survey to distribute to others to determine their interest level in your selected project. Be sure to include the following in your survey:
   ▸ What is the project or activity?
   ▸ What are the objectives of the project?
   ▸ What is the interest level in the project?
   ▸ Who might be interested in participating actively in the project?
   ▸ Give a date for the survey to be returned to you.

9. Collect the surveys, and analyze the findings. Make a recommendation to your school administration. If your team recommends implementing the project at your school, volunteer to be involved in a leadership role to get the project started at your school.

10. Communicate with NASSP to let them know the status of your school's involvement in the project.

Activity 10
Selling on the Net

Do you know about the Consumer Bill of Rights?

As the number of Internet users increases, business on the Internet continues to grow. More and more consumers access the Internet and explore catalogs and advertisements for products and services. As a consumer you have rights that provide for honest and fair treatment from businesses—including businesses on the Internet.

Are you an informed Internet consumer? Are you aware of all the correct information about each product or service you are considering to buy? Are you willing to transfer your credit card number through cyberspace? How do you know whether a business on the Internet is legitimate or whether the Net ad is a "cyber-scam"? These questions and more are typical of Internet users who want to become better informed.

After you complete this activity, you will be able to:

- Use a search engine to locate retail information on the Internet.
- Identify secure and unsecure systems using your browser.
- Identify potential dangers associated with security on the Internet.
- Browse retail sales data on the Internet.
- Compose a brief essay.

To learn about retail sales on the Internet, let's explore.

1. Choose one of these product areas to research for retail information on the Internet.
   - ▶ books
   - ▶ music
   - ▶ computers

2. Begin your exploration by launching your browser.

Many retail sites provide search tools and links to product descriptions, vendor information, and online ordering. Scroll home pages before linking to another page.

3. Go to the appropriate sites to search for retail information about the product area you chose:

Books, music, or computers:	Branch Mall	**http://branch.com/**
Books:	Amazon.com	**http://www.amazon.com/**
Music:	CD Now	**http://cdnow.com/**
Computers:	Internet Shopping Network	**http://www.internet.net/**

Note: If you want to search for additional retail sites related to your chosen product area, you may use a search engine at one of these sites:

Search engines allow you to search on the Internet for information on a particular topic.

AltaVista	**http://www.altavista.digital.com/**
Lycos	**http://www.lycos.com/**
Yahoo	**http://www.yahoo.com/**
Excite	**http://www.excite.com/**
Magellan	**http://www.mckinley.com/**

You may link to and
view order information
pages, but do **not** place
an order.

4. Search for information about your selected product area, linking to the pages that interest you.

5. As you browse the web, observe the security level of the pages. Notice an icon, such as a lock or key, at the bottom of your screen as shown in Figures 2-12 and 2-13.

Figure 2-12
Unsecure Document

| Document Done | |

Figure 2-13
Secure Document

| Document Done | |

In an **unsecure** document, information is accessible to other people. In a **secure** document, however, confidential information, such as a credit card number, is encrypted so that others may not access it. You may display security status of a document by clicking on the icons.

Note: A broken key, for example, represents an unsecure document, and a solid key represents a secure document. Most often you will see unsecure documents until you are actually ready to place an order.

6. On a separate sheet of paper, record a few secure and unsecure pages you may locate.

   ▶ What products are the secure pages offering via the Internet?
   ▶ What products are the unsecure pages offering via the Internet?

7. Exit your browser.

8. Using your word processing software, compose a brief essay describing your perspective of security and the Internet. Consider these questions:

   ▶ What did you learn about retail sales on the Internet?
   ▶ Would you feel comfortable ordering a product on the Internet?
   ▶ Should you use a credit card number on the Internet?
   ▶ How are security issues affecting retail business on the Internet?

Activity 11
Shopping for a Computer

Computers are everywhere—in businesses, hospitals, churches, schools, and homes. Computers allow us to process data quickly, to store information, and to access information more efficiently. Many of our daily activities involve a computer. Think about your last visit to a bank, a restaurant, a retail store, a car dealership, a college campus, an amusement park, or a gas station. Undoubtedly you saw employees and customers using computers everywhere you visited. With the widespread use of computers, we can't imagine life without them.

If your family has a computer at home, think of all the ways each member of your family has become accustomed to using it. Is your computer powerful enough to handle all the tasks your family wants to accomplish? What additional equipment do you need to have a more powerful computer? If you do not have a computer at home, what benefits would your family gain from owning a computer?

Whether your family is considering the purchase of a newer, more powerful computer or your first computer, talk to each member of your family to learn how each would use the computer. As an example, does your family want to access the Internet? If so, you need a modem. After you know your family's wish list, learn all you can about computers, different models and vendors, software, and related costs. You will then be better able to define your specific computer needs and make a well-informed recommendation to your family.

After you complete this activity, you will be able to:

- Define basic computer terms.
- Make an informed recommendation about purchasing a computer.
- Prepare a database and a database report to use for comparison shopping.
- Orally discuss your research findings and recommendations.

To learn about computer systems and buying direct, let's explore the Internet.

1. Begin your exploration by launching your browser.

2. Go to the *Computer Shopper* site at this URL:
   http://www.zdnet.com/cshopper/
   Note: Scroll down this page, and note the various categories of information.

3. The *Computer Shopper* home page on your screen should be similar to Figure 2-14 on page 52. At this site you will browse the Internet and read appropriate articles to help you define basic computer terms, learn about buying direct, define your specific computer needs, and understand computer performance.

Figure 2-14
Computer Shopper Home Page

Surfing the Net is time-consuming. As you browse, however, take time to read articles so you will be able to make your computer recommendation.

To help you get started with your exploration on the *Computer Shopper* page, link to Smart Shopper: Buying Advice. Then link to Expert Tips, and explore the links on this page to learn about buying direct and technical support. Continue browsing until you find information about two different computer systems.

Note: As you conduct research, remember to record *complete* information about two different computer systems on a separate sheet of paper. Also, find and record the definition of these basic computer terms: *pc*, *processor (CPU)*, *RAM*, *ROM*, *hard drive*, *Megahertz (MHz)*, and *modem*. You may also want to ask your teacher whether you may print articles or save them to disk for later reference.

Search for computer-related articles to read.

4. If you want to read more articles about buying computers, consider these articles (or search for other articles):
   "I give up: what should I buy?" at **http://www.mont.mindspring.com/~jtu3/arts/95.09.11whattobuy.html** and "Scanning for Bargains" at **http://www.mont.mindspring.com/~jtu3/arts/96.05.06bargains.html**

5. Based on your research, review and update your family's computer needs.
   ▸ Have you identified two computer systems that will meet your family's needs?

6. Go back to the *Computer Shopper* home page and link to Smart Shopper: Shopping Tools. Then link to NetBuyer to begin your comparison shopping. Explore the links on this page to shop for specific products, research for more advice, and do side-by-side comparisons. Browse these pages, and have fun shopping!
   Note: The Side by Side Comparisons page provides an excellent means to see the differences between systems quickly and easily.

You may link to and view order information pages, but do **not** place an order.

7. Continue browsing the Internet until you secure complete pricing information for two computer systems that meet your family's needs. You may also explore competitive information by going to one of the computer retail sites at these URLs:

Internet Shopping Network	**http://www.internet.net/**
MicroWarehouse, Inc.	**http://www.warehouse.com/**
Computer Warehouse	**http://usashopping.com/cgi-win/cw/ cwnet.exe**
L & H Computers	**http://www.citivu.com/rc/lnh/ index.html**

8. Exit your browser.

9. Using your database software, prepare a database with the information you secured about the two different computer systems. You may want to include fields in your database such as processor, RAM, maximum RAM, hard disk size, MHz (speed), CD-ROM speed, modem speed, monitor included, monitor size, and price.

   Note: You may also want to prepare a database report with an appropriate report heading to display your findings.

10. In an assigned team, compare and analyze all data collected.

    ▶ Outline the computer needs of your family and your recommendations.

    ▶ What is the most important information to consider in purchasing a computer?

    ▶ How might you use the Internet for shopping purposes in the future?

Activity 12
Analyzing Census Data

The United States has recently been called a "salad bowl" because it is a colorful mix of different people. Americans take pride in their diverse cultural backgrounds and heritage without feeling as if they have to "blend in" with everyone else. This cultural diversity is reflected in the census data gathered by the government.

The United States Census Bureau takes a **census**—an official counting of the people—every ten years. The census data provides more than just population figures. The agency collects demographic data about people, such as age, race, marital status, education, and employment. It also gathers economic indicators on housing starts, retail sales, exports, and many other areas.

By analyzing census data, we can learn about the population of our country and the economic conditions that affect everyone. Studying the data helps us to identify trends and plan for our future.

After you complete this activity, you will be able to:

- Locate census data for population, earnings, and economic indicators.
- Compare census data.
- Describe the increased benefits of higher educational attainment.
- Learn more about the occurrence of first and last names in this country.
- Create a survey.
- Create and sort a database.
- Compose a memo about your research.

To learn more about analyzing census data, let's explore the Internet.

1. Launch your browser to begin your exploration.

The top-level domain gov identifies the U.S. Census Bureau site as a government web site.

2. Go to the U.S. Census Bureau web site at this URL:
   http://www.census.gov/
   Your screen should be similar to the U.S. Census Bureau home page in Figure 2-15 on page 55.

You may want to save, print, or copy/paste the information you locate to help you compose your report for this activity.

3. Link to <u>About the Bureau</u>. Review the mission, customer service standards, and background of this government agency.
   ▸ What is the mission of the United States Census Bureau?
   ▸ What is the background of the United States Census Bureau?
   ▸ Approximately how many statistical reports does the United States Census Bureau issue during a census year?
   ▸ How does this agency distribute the data it collects?

4. Go back to the U.S. Census Bureau home page.

5. Link to <u>Current U.S. Population Count</u> to review the population clocks (or POP Clocks) for the United States and the world.

Figure 2-15
U.S. Census Bureau Home Page

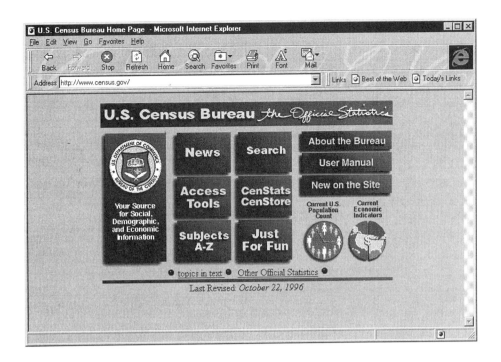

> ▶ What is the estimated population of the United States?
> ▶ What is the projected world population today?
> ▶ What factors affect the population in our country?
> ▶ Do all of the same factors apply to the entire world?

6. Go back to the U.S. Census Bureau home page. Link to <u>Subjects A–Z</u>, and then to the <u>Education</u> subject area. Locate the most recent census data that reflects the mean earnings of workers eighteen years or older based on educational attainment.

> ▶ Based on the most recent data, what is the mean (average) earnings for a high school graduate (both sexes)?
> ▶ What is the mean earnings for someone who is not a high school graduate (both sexes)?
> ▶ Determine the difference between the two mean earnings, and calculate the percentage difference.
> ▶ What is the percentage difference between the mean earnings of a high school graduate and a college graduate with a bachelor's degree?
> ▶ Explain why someone with a college degree may earn more than a typical high school graduate.

7. From Subjects A–Z, link to the <u>Genealogy</u> subject area. Locate information on frequently occurring names.

> ▶ What is the most common surname (or last name) in the United States?
> ▶ What is the most common female first name?
> ▶ What is the most common male first name?
> ▶ Where does your surname rank?
> *Note:* Search the Names files to find where your last name ranks instead of trying to find your surname in the directory list. The entire last name directory could take several minutes to appear since it contains almost 90,000 names.

Remember that you can stop the transfer of data to your computer if too much information exists.

8. Go back to the U.S. Census Bureau home page.
   ▶ What is the estimated current population count for the United States?
   ▶ How much has this estimate changed since you last checked it?

9. Link to Current Economic Indicators from the home page. Link to Retail Sales. Review the latest retail sales news, and analyze the estimated monthly retail sales graph.
   ▶ Have the monthly estimated retail sales increased or decreased over the previous twelve months?
   ▶ Approximately how much has this indicator changed over this period?
   ▶ What has been the trend in retail sales over the past three years?

10. Exit your browser.

11. In your assigned team, create and distribute a survey to gather demographic information about your class. For example, the survey could include questions to determine how many children are in each student's family and how many telephones and televisions are in each household.

12. Using your database software, create a statistical database to organize the data. Set up the required fields, for example, Family Name, Children, Telephones, and Televisions. Record the data you collected on the survey. Calculate the mean, median, and mode for the demographic data.
    Note: Sort the data by the various demographics to help you find the mode and median statistics.

13. Using your word processing software, compose a memo to your teacher to summarize your team's findings.

Activity 13
Tracking Stock Quotes

Since your childhood have your parents and others encouraged you to save or invest some of your money? You may have opened a savings account, saved a few dollars, and earned some interest. Did you consider buying shares of stock as a way to invest some of your money? While the risk may be higher to buy stock than to put money in a savings account, the return on your investment may be considerably higher.

If you want to invest some money in stocks, you can go to a stockbroker. The stockbroker will recommend which stock to purchase and actually process the transaction for you—for a fee. Then if you ever want to sell the stock, the stockbroker will process the transaction for you—again, for a fee.

You can use telecommunications to view daily stock quotes.

How can you use telecommunications to help you determine which stock to purchase? Each day millions and millions of data related to the stock market are transferred via telecommunications. The current listings of the stock market transfers are known as **quotes**. Telecommunications services update quotes every fifteen minutes while the stock market is open for trading.

With access to the Internet, you can conduct research about selected companies, read news articles related to the particular companies, and actually track stock market quotes. With your research you will be better prepared to choose a company in which to invest money.

After you complete this activity, you will be able to:

- Search for news-related articles about major companies.
- Research for information about the stock market.
- Gather current stock market quotes for a specific time period.
- Compose a research report.

To learn about the stock market and to locate stock market quotes, let's explore the Internet.

1. Begin your exploration of stock market data by launching your browser.

2. Go to the Yahoo search engine site at this URL:
   http://www.yahoo.com/

The top-level domain com identifies the Yahoo site as a commercial service web site.

3. Link to <u>Today's News</u>, and then explore the business <u>Headlines</u> page. *Note:* This page has links to business news stories that are appearing in the headlines.

4. Explore the links on this page to research current news articles about companies. Look for articles related to financial news, such as sales, mergers, or buyouts; changes in the senior-level officers; expanding markets, product lines, or services; restructurings, downsizings, or hirings; or an announcement about a private company going public.

   ▶ What companies are in the leading news stories?

5. From your research of the articles, identify at least two companies that you want to study. On a separate sheet of paper, record the name of each company. Based on your research of the articles, also record what you think might occur to the stock for each of the companies during the next few months.
   Note: Your teacher will tell you how long you will conduct research on these companies.

6. Go back to the business headlines page, and link to <u>Company</u>. You will now be able to research for specific background information or a profile on each company you want to study.
   Note: The information is arranged alphabetically by company name.

7. For each company you have selected, explore the news, profile, and quote.

8. Go to a stock quote web site such as RealTime Quotes at **http://www.rtquotes.com/** and explore links to articles and quotes.
   Note: You may also want to consider a stock quote web site at one of these URLs:

Pathfinder	**http://pathfinder.com/money/quote/qc**
NASDAQ	**http://www.nasdaq.com/**
Yahoo Stock Quotes	**http://quote.yahoo.com/**

9. Move forward through the links to the input link, as shown in Figure 2-16 for RealTime Quotes. Enter the ticker symbol for the stock market quote of your choice.
   Note: If you do not know the ticker symbol for the stock quote that you want, move forward to the search link that will allow you to enter the company name to learn the correct ticker symbol. Be sure to record

Figure 2-16
RealTime Quotes Page

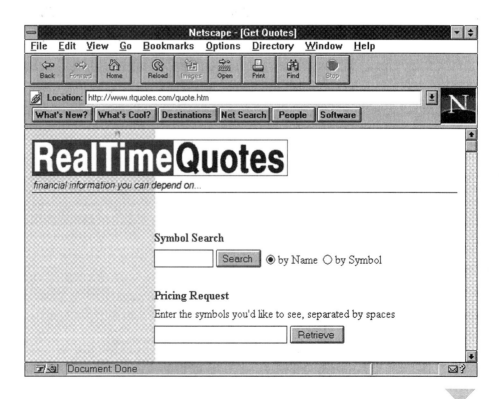

the ticker symbol in your journal for each of the companies you are researching.

10. On a separate sheet of paper, record the stock quote for each of the two companies you are researching.

11. Exit your browser.

Take time to study stock market quotes for a company so you can determine the value of the company.

12. To see and evaluate changes in stock quotes, you must secure quotes over a given time period. The longer you research the companies, the more information you will have to make your decision about whether you would invest in them. Secure the stock quote each day for the time period your teacher has assigned.

13. Using spreadsheet software, plan a spreadsheet similar to the worksheet below to record your stock market quotes for each of the companies over the given time period. Enter formulas to indicate the changes over time.

Stock Market Quotes							
Ticker Symbol	Day 1*	Change	Day 2	Change	Day 3	Change	Change from Day 1 to Day 3

*In the column headings, use the appropriate word for the time you secured the quotes (for example, *Day* or *Week*). Include a column for each time you secured the quotes.

14. In your assigned team, share information on the results of your research. Include the following information:

▶ What companies did you research?
▶ In which company would you recommend investing money? Why?
▶ How should you select stocks for long-term investments?

Activity 14
Tracking Pro Teams to Playoff Time

Who will win the pennant? Which teams made it to the Super Bowl? What about the Stanley Cup? We can't forget the NBA Championship. Are your predictions at the beginning of the season going to last through the playoffs?

You can use the Internet to track team statistics, read the latest sports news, review player salaries, or just learn more about your favorite sports team. Several web sites provide coverage for different sports, such as hockey, tennis, golf, baseball, football, and basketball. Some professional sports associations (Major League Baseball, for example) have their own official web site with in-depth information about every team and the players.

After you complete this activity, you will be able to:

- Search for news regarding professional sports teams.
- Gather data on team statistics and standings.
- Evaluate data to report the findings.
- Compose a report about your research.

To learn more about a sports team, let's explore the Internet.

1. Launch your browser to begin your exploration.

The top-level domain **com** identifies the NBA site as a commercial service web site.

2. Go to the NBA (National Basketball Association) web site at this URL: **http://www.nba.com/**
   Your screen should be similar to the NBA home page in Figure 2-17 on page 61.

3. Link to <u>Scores & Stats</u> and then to <u>Team-by-Team</u> to find statistics on a team-by-team basis.
   ▶ Who has the highest points per game (PPG) average for the Boston Celtics?
   ▶ Which player has the highest free throw percentage (FT%) for the Chicago Bulls?
   ▶ Who has the best field goal percentage (FG%) for the Los Angeles Lakers?
   ▶ List five players for the Orlando Magic.

   If you are completing this activity during the off-season, answer the following questions instead of those given above.
   ▶ Which team won the NBA championship last year?
   ▶ Which team was the runner-up?

4. Link to <u>Current Regular Season</u> from the Scores and Stats page.
   ▶ Which team is leading the Atlantic Conference?
   ▶ What is this team's win/loss percentage?
   ▶ Which team is leading the Central Conference?

Figure 2-17
NBA Home Page

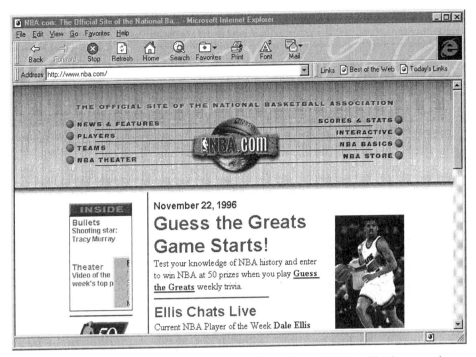

You may want to save, print, or copy/paste the information you locate to help you compose your report for this activity.

Remember to enter the URL exactly as shown.

5. From the NBA home page, link to data about a basketball team or player. Record information regarding current statistics, team facts, and career highlights.

6. Browse these web sites for professional and collegiate sports information about a sports team or player for your report for this activity:

National Hockey League	http://www.nhl.com/
National Football League	http://www.nfl.com/
National Basketball Association	http://www.nba.com/
Major League Baseball	http://www.majorleaguebaseball.com/
The Sports Network	http://sportsnetwork.com/
ESPN	http://espn.com/
NBC Sports	http://nbc.com/sports/

7. Exit your browser.

8. Using your word processing or desktop publishing software, compose a one-page report about a sports team or a player.

Activity 15
Choosing a College

For many years you have undoubtedly been asked this question: What do you want to be when you grow up? More than likely, when you have considered this question seriously, you may have had a different answer at different times. Regardless of what you want to be someday, you will probably need education beyond high school. You may want to attend a two-year school (a community or junior college) or a four-year college or university.

Carefully research answers to many questions before you choose a college.

The college you attend and the type of degree you earn will influence many decisions throughout your life. Furthermore, the reputation of the college in your major area of study may affect your future career opportunities and earning potential. Before you choose a college, you should consider many factors, including the name of the college and its reputation in the area you want to pursue, the location of the college, the annual cost to attend the college, the types of financial assistance available, the application process, and the selection criteria for those who are accepted to the college.

Learn all you can about different colleges and universities and what they have to offer so you will be able to make an informed decision about where to attend college.

After you complete this activity, you will be able to:

- Find information related to choosing a college.
- Search for specific colleges that meet your criteria.
- Make an informed decision about which college to attend.
- Create a database.

To learn about colleges in the United States and abroad, let's explore the Internet.

1. Launch your browser to begin your exploration of colleges.

The top-level domain *edu* identifies the Bates College site as an education web site.

2. Go to the Bates College Online home page at this URL: **http://www.bates.edu/**

3. Link to <u>Admissions</u>, and then link to <u>College checklists for juniors and seniors</u>. As shown in Figure 2-18 on page 63, the College Selection Checklist should appear on your screen. Read the College Selection Checklist to learn about the exploration process to find a college, the timing of events, and the application process.

> ▶ Analyze where you are in your college search process.
> ▶ Identify what you should be doing at this time.

Choosing a college is a serious decision that involves much time and research.

4. Consider the questions you have about going to college. Do you know which colleges offer a degree in your interest area? Do you know how to choose a college or how you will pay for your college education? Don't be discouraged by all the questions you have; you are not alone. You

Figure 2-18
College Selection Checklist Page

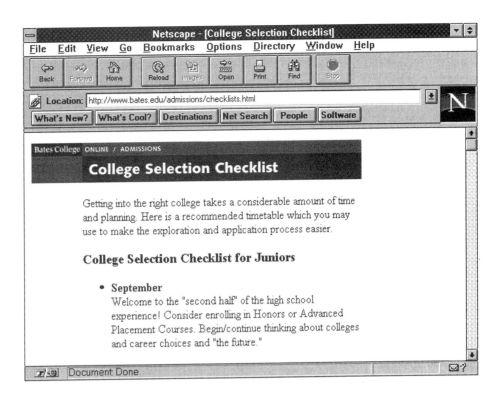

Netscape - [College Selection Checklist]

File Edit View Go Bookmarks Options Directory Window Help

Back Forward Home Reload Images Open Print Find Stop

Location: http://www.bates.edu/admissions/checklists.html

What's New? What's Cool? Destinations Net Search People Software

Bates College ONLINE / ADMISSIONS

College Selection Checklist

Getting into the right college takes a considerable amount of time and planning. Here is a recommended timetable which you may use to make the exploration and application process easier.

College Selection Checklist for Juniors

- **September**
  Welcome to the "second half" of the high school experience! Consider enrolling in Honors or Advanced Placement Courses. Begin/continue thinking about colleges and career choices and "the future."

Document Done

The top-level domain gov identifies the U.S. Department of Education site as a government site.

may find the answers to some of your questions and definitions for the most frequently used terms by exploring information at the U.S. Department of Education web site at this URL: **http://www.ed.gov/**

5. At the U.S. Department of Education web site, link first to <u>Publications & Products</u> and then to <u>Publications for Parents</u>. Even though this site is for parents, you can benefit from a visit here. Scroll down this page, and link to the publication <u>*Preparing Your Child for College*</u>. Browse the information that interests you.

   ▶ Did you find the answers to your questions about going to college?
   ▶ Based on what you read, should you plan to attend college to prepare for the career you want to pursue?
   ▶ What steps should you take to choose a college?
   ▶ How will you go about financing your college education?
   ▶ Identify the terms for which you found an explanation.
   ▶ Are there any questions you should ask your guidance counselor?

The top-level domain org identifies the Job-Web site as an organization site.

6. Are you ready to search for a college to attend? Go to the Catapult Visiting Colleges and Universities page at this URL: **http://www.jobweb.org/catapult/colleges.htm** *Note:* Scroll down the page, and note the links you may want to explore as your time allows.

7. Link to <u>CollegeNet</u> to explore for institutions by criteria, such as geography and enrollments. Then link to <u>College Search</u> and <u>Four-Year U.S. Colleges</u> to explore for specific colleges. *Note:* You may want to return to this page to explore the information for community, technical, and junior colleges.

8. Use the CollegeNet search engine to explore for your ideal institution. CollegeNet will search for schools based on your criteria related to the states, enrollment, tuition, name of school, type of school, majors offered, and intercollegiate sports offered. CollegeNet will sort the list of schools meeting your criteria alphabetically, by state, by enrollment, tuition, and so on. Scroll down the page, and enter the appropriate information. Then process your search request.

   Note: If the result of your search is "no matches for your criteria," return to the CollegeNet Search Engine page and change your criteria. If the result of your search is an extremely large number of colleges, you may want to return to the CollegeNet Search Engine page and limit your criteria to narrow the results.

   ▶ What schools are identified that meet your criteria?

9. Link to specific information about the schools that interest you. *Note:* Some institutions offer a link to send an e-mail message. Ask your teacher whether you may do so to request more information.

   ▶ What did you learn about the institution, the academic programs, the admission process and requirements, the tuition, and student life?

Use your browser to "go" directly to a previously viewed page.

10. If desired, go back to the College Search page, and perform other searches with different information.

11. Exit your browser.

12. Using your database software, prepare a database of the information you secured about the colleges that interest you, including fields such as Institution, Tuition per Year, ACT/SAT Score Required, City/State, Offers My Intended Major.

13. Analyze your findings.

    ▶ What college best meets your requirements?
    ▶ Should you conduct more research?
    ▶ What is your next step to choose a college?

Activity 16
Evaluating Your Personality

Are you an intuitive person? Do you make decisions based on how you feel? Are you a good judge of character? Do you plan your activities, or are you spontaneous? Would you describe yourself as outgoing or shy? Do you prefer to work alone or with others? Do your personality traits make a difference when you are considering various careers?

Career and guidance counselors often administer a personality test to help individuals think about their common behaviors. The test results help people understand who they are and how they relate to others in personal and business situations. And, as you learn more about yourself by studying the test results, you should be able to better evaluate whether your personality traits match a particular career.

One of the popular "personality" tests available on the Internet is The Keirsey Temperament Sorter. Anyone can take this interactive personality test and then analyze the personality traits related to the test score.

After you complete this activity, you will be able to:

- Take an interactive personality test.
- Describe how personality traits may be linked to career choices.
- Analyze your results from the personality test, and evaluate the degree of accuracy in your test scores.

To learn about your personality traits, let's explore the Internet.

1. Launch your browser to begin your exploration.

2. Go to The Keirsey Temperament Sorter page at this URL:
   http://sunsite.unc.edu/personality/keirsey.html
   Your screen should be similar to the web page in Figure 2-19 on page 66.

The top-level domain *edu* identifies The Keirsey Temperament Sorter page as an education site.

3. Read the information on this page, and link to <u>Take the test</u>.
   Note: You can take The Keirsey Temperament Sorter personality test online. Each of the seventy questions has two choices. There are no right or wrong answers to the questions. Instead, try to give the answer that is the most typical result for you. The more honest your responses are, the more reliable your test results will be.

Scroll through the information to see the entire page and the hypertext link.

4. Answer all the questions on the personality test. Then link to <u>Score test</u>.

5. After you score your test, the results will appear as four line charts. The charts indicate your ratings in four areas: Extrovert versus Introvert, Sensation versus Intuitive, Thinking versus Feeling, and Judging versus Perceiving.

At the bottom of the page, your score is identified with four letters. Each letter represents a basic personality trait. Record these four letters on a piece of paper.

Figure 2-19
The Keirsey Temperament
Sorter Page

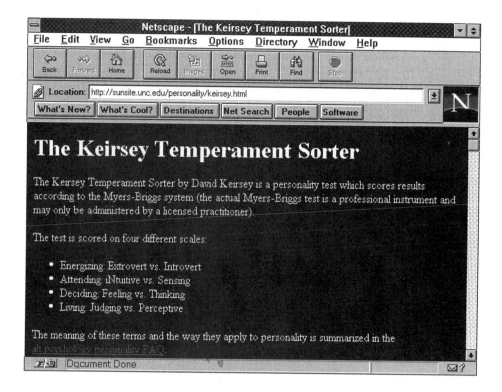

The Keirsey Temperament Sorter

The Keirsey Temperament Sorter by David Keirsey is a personality test which scores results according to the Myers-Briggs system (the actual Myers-Briggs test is a professional instrument and may only be administered by a licensed practitioner).

The test is scored on four different scales:

- Energizing: Extrovert vs. Introvert
- Attending: iNtuitive vs. Sensing
- Deciding: Feeling vs. Thinking
- Living: Judging vs. Perceptive

The meaning of these terms and the way they apply to personality is summarized in the alt psychology personality FAQ.

6. To learn the meaning of your score, link to the four-letter score at the bottom of your screen. Read the profile of individuals with these personality traits.

   ▶ Does this profile describe you accurately?
   ▶ What other famous people had this personality type?

Use your browser to "go" directly to a previously view page.

7. Go back to The Keirsey Temperament Test Results page, and link to the words in the line charts that represent your score. For example, if your score is *ISFJ*, explore Introvert, Sensation, Feeling, and Judging.

   ▶ What is the definition of each trait represented in your four-letter score?

8. Scroll to the information on Preferred Vocabulary for each of the Four Scales. Read the information that relates to your score.

   ▶ Identify several descriptors for each of the four letters of your score. For example, if you scored as an extrovert, a preferred term is *interaction*.

9. Scroll to A Short Summary of the Sixteen Personality Types, and read the information that relates to your score.

   ▶ What is the summary of your score?

10. Exit your browser.

11. In your assigned team, discuss the accuracy of your personality test results. Also explore why many employers are now giving a personality test to their employees and potential employees.

Activity 17
Choosing Automobile Insurance

Could you afford to have your car repaired if you were involved in an automobile accident? What if you were injured or you damaged someone else's property in an accident? Automobile insurance is one type of insurance that protects you from financial losses if you are involved in an accident.

These six basic automobile insurance options provide coverage to pay losses that could result from an accident: bodily injury liability, property damage liability, medical payments, collision, comprehensive, and uninsured motorists.

The Insurance News Network site provides information about life, home, and automobile insurance. You can use this site to learn more about coverage options, to compare rates among insurance carriers, and to determine ways to reduce your insurance premiums.

After you complete this activity, you will be able to:

- Define the different types of automobile insurance.
- Explain why insurance rates vary for different vehicles.
- Identify factors, such as vehicle safety and theft rates, that affect the cost of insurance.
- Define automobile insurance requirements for your state.
- Compose a report about your research.

To learn more about automobile insurance, let's explore the Internet.

1. Launch your browser to begin your exploration.

2. Go to the Insurance News Network web site at this URL:
   http://www.insure.com/
   Your screen should be similar to the Insurance News Network home page in Figure 2-20 on page 68.

Sometimes you may have to scroll through information to see the entire page and the hypertext links.

3. Link to the <u>Auto</u> or <u>Auto Insurance</u> page. Locate and explore the different kinds of insurance coverage.
   - Which insurance coverage pays for damages to your vehicle?
   - How can you reduce the cost of collision coverage?
   - Which option pays for damage due to theft, vandalism, or a natural disaster?
   - How can you protect yourself if you have an accident with someone who does not have any coverage?
   - Identify a few discounts that insurance companies offer.

4. How much should you pay for insurance? Link to the information about average annual automobile premiums.
   Note: Remember that the content and links on a web page may change at any time. When you explore a page looking for information, try to

Figure 2-20
Insurance News Network
Home Page

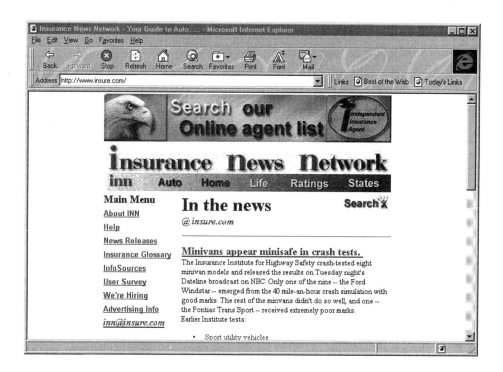

find links that match your search criteria. Sometimes they are not obvious. For example, to find the average annual premiums, look for a link such as How much should I pay? or Rates. Then explore that page and other links for the information you need.

▶ Based on the most recent data, which state has the highest average rate?

▶ Which state has the lowest average rate?

▶ Where does your state rank?

You may want to save, print, or copy/paste the information you locate to help you compose your report for this activity.

5. Go back to Insurance News Network—Auto. Explore how insurance rates are affected by the type of car you drive and where you live.

▶ Would the type of car and where you live affect your insurance premiums?

▶ Which type of car is most likely to be stolen?

▶ What are the top five cities with the highest automobile theft rates?

6. From Insurance News Network—Auto, link to State Information. Explore your state's insurance department web site via the NAIC Map and Hotlink page. (Choose any other state if your state does not have a site.)

Note: The National Association of Insurance Commissioners (NAIC) is a group representing all the state insurance departments. This organization has a web site (URL: **http://www.naic.org/**) with links to the individual state insurance department sites.

▶ What minimum insurance requirements does your state impose?

▶ Why do states set certain insurance requirements?

Instead of going back through several pages, use your browser to "go" directly to a previously viewed page.

7. Go back to the Insurance News Network—Auto page. Research the process to file a claim if you were in an automobile accident.

   ▶ Identify the steps to follow if you are involved in an accident.

8. Exit your browser.

9. Using your word processing or desktop publishing software, compose a report that summarizes your findings. Topics may include the following:

   ▶ Why should you purchase insurance?
   ▶ What factors would influence your decision as to which insurance carrier you should choose?
   ▶ What coverage options are essential?
   ▶ Are some options not required?
   ▶ What should you do if you are in an accident?

Activity 18
Buying a Car

Are you able to go where you want without asking someone for transportation? We all want wheels, don't we? Do you want a new Mercedes but don't have quite enough cash to pay for such an expensive model? If you're like most people, you would probably need to use credit to get that car.

Buying your first car could be confusing if you're not familiar with such terms as *APR (annual percentage rate)*, *principal*, and *repayment period*. Being an educated consumer can help you decide whether you can afford a brand new Mercedes or a second-hand car.

Before you borrow money from a lender, such as a bank or a credit union, you should know the cost of using credit. What's the APR? How much will you have to pay per month? Several bank web sites, such as the one maintained by The Toronto-Dominion Bank (or TD Bank), include loan calculators to assist you in computing loan payments.

After you complete this activity, you will be able to:

- Make a more informed decision about the financial aspects of purchasing a car.
- Search for information related to car loans.
- Prepare a spreadsheet to calculate total interest payments.
- Create a spreadsheet chart (a bar graph) to compare interest costs.

To learn more about calculating loan payments, let's explore the Internet.

1. Launch your browser to begin your exploration.

> **The top-level domain *ca* represents a Canadian web site.**

2. Go to the TD Bank (or The Toronto-Dominion Bank) web site at this URL: **http://www.tdbank.ca/**
   Your screen should be similar to the TD Bank home page in Figure 2-21 on page 71.

3. Link to <u>Search the TD Site!</u>, then enter **loan calculator** as the search keywords, and process your request to locate the loan calculator. Use the search results to go to the page with the loan calculator.
   Note: Exploring a site in search of information can feel like trying to find a "needle in a haystack." When available, use the search engine a site provides to help you locate information quickly and easily.

4. Suppose you want to finance $7,500 towards the purchase of a car. What is the monthly payment if the annual percentage rate (APR) is 11 percent and the repayment period is three years? Use the loan calculator to compute the monthly payment.
   ▶ What is the total cash outlay (monthly payments times the number of payments) over the entire loan period?

Figure 2-21
TD Bank Home Page

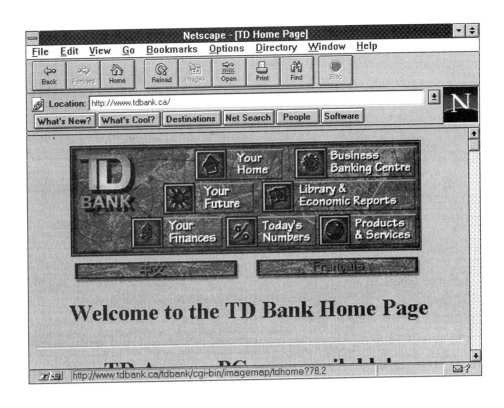

> How much interest (total cash outlay minus loan amount) would you pay for this loan?
> What is the monthly payment at 10 percent APR?

5. Use the loan calculator to determine your monthly payment to finance $14,500 at 12 percent APR for 36 months.

> Would the monthly payment be lower if you financed the loan for 48 months?
> Why is the monthly payment different for a longer time period?

6. Calculate the monthly payment on a $10,000 loan financed for 36 months at the following annual percentage rates: 5, 7, 9, 11, and 13 percent. Record your results.

You may use your browser to "go" directly to a previously viewed page.

7. Go back to the TD Bank home page.

> Does the TD Bank web site provide multilingual support? If so, what languages are available?
> Why does a Canadian bank provide information in different languages?

8. Exit your browser.

9. Using your spreadsheet software, create a spreadsheet that shows the monthly payments, total payments over the entire loan period, and the total interest paid for each of the interest rates identified in step 6. (See the sample worksheet on page 72.)

INTEREST RATE COMPUTATIONS

Loan Amount	$10,000	10,000	10,000	10,000	10,000
Repayment Period	3	3	3	3	3
APR	5%	7%	9%	11%	13%
Monthly Payment					
Total Payments					
Total Interest					

10. Analyze your spreadsheet.

    ▶ How much more total interest would you pay for the $10,000 loan at 11 percent versus 5 percent?
    ▶ Why should you compare interest rates before financing a car?

11. Create a bar chart that reflects the total interest paid at each interest rate.

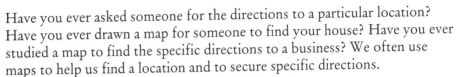

Activity 19
Mapping Your Way

Have you ever asked someone for the directions to a particular location? Have you ever drawn a map for someone to find your house? Have you ever studied a map to find the specific directions to a business? We often use maps to help us find a location and to secure specific directions.

Cartography, the study of maps, helps us learn about our history and geography. For instance, just how were the state's boundaries decided? Why were roads built where they were? Have you ever noticed that some maps have different colors that depict elevation differences, such as mountains and valleys? We can learn different things from the various types of maps.

After you complete this activity, you will be able to:

- Plot a specific location on a map.
- Use the Internet to secure a map (if you have a graphical browser) and driving directions.
- Send an e-mail message with a map.
- Use numerous criteria to search for locations.
- Determine the distance between two points.
- Explain the purposes of cartography.
- Analyze your findings.

To learn about maps, let's explore the Internet.

1. Launch your browser to begin your exploration.

2. Go to the Lycos home page at this URL: **http://www.lycos.com/**

3. Link to <u>Road Maps</u>. Your screen should be similar to the Road Maps page in Figure 2-22 on page 74.

4. In the appropriate fields, type this address: **1600 Pennsylvania Avenue, Washington, DC.** Then process the search request.

5. When the list appears with one or more locations resulting from the search, link to the location that is closest to the address you entered.

6. Study the map that appears on the Map Navigation page (if you have a graphical browser). Note in particular where the exact address is located. Explore the various options to change the perspective of the map.
   Note: Use the key below the map to explore the various map views. For instance, you can zoom in on a section of the map.
   ▸ How does the feature to change the map view help you?

7. Link to <u>New Location</u>. In the appropriate fields, type your street address, city, state, and ZIP code. Then process your search request, and link to the map.

A search engine will allow you to search on the Internet for information.

Access Lycos Map help to review the tips for navigating.

Figure 2-22
RoadMaps Page

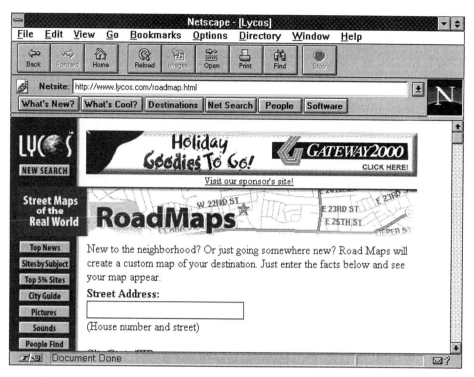

FAQs refer to a page that contains questions and answers.

▶ Is the map accurate?

▶ Why might the address not be completely on target? (You may want to access *Frequently Asked Questions* from the **Help** menu to explore the reasons.)

8. *Optional:* Would you like to send a friend or relative a copy of the map for the area near where you live? Scroll to the commands at the bottom of the Map Navigation page. Link to <u>Mail</u>. In the appropriate fields, type the e-mail address for the person you want to send a copy of your map, your e-mail address, and your message. Then send your mail message.
   Note: You may want to use the suggested message on the web page. If the recipient's mail reader supports MIME (as does Netscape and Microsoft Internet Explorer), mark the appropriate field before you mail the message.

Use your browser to "go" directly to a previously viewed page.

9. Would you like to have specific driving directions from one place to another? Go back to the Lycos RoadMaps page, and link to <u>driving directions</u>. Read the information on this page.

10. In the appropriate fields, type the address for the starting point, and then set the starting point. Verify the information on the next screen.

11. In the appropriate fields, type the address for your destination, and then set the destination.

12. Link to the type of trip you prefer, and review the map that appears.
    ▶ Does the map look accurate?
    ▶ Are the step-by-step directions correct and helpful?

▶ How many miles are between your starting point and your destination?

Note: Ask your teacher whether you may print the driving directions.

13. Suppose you want to "map out" a list of Internet providers for your geographical area. Go to the Yahoo home page at this URL: **http://www.yahoo.com/**
Link to U.S. States. Then continue linking to Cities, your state, Internet Services, and finally Internet Access Providers. You should see a list of ISPs for your area.

   ▶ How many ISPs are in your area?
   ▶ Identify two of the ISPs.

14. Now let's find the distance between two locations. Go back to the Yahoo home page, and link to Regional. Then continue the linking process to Geography, Geographic Information Systems, and Distance between two locations. The How far is it? page should appear on your screen.

15. Type information in the appropriate fields to secure the distance between the city where you live and Washington, DC. Process the search, and then explore the links on the Distance Result page.

   ▶ How many miles is it to Washington, DC from your house?
   ▶ In what general direction will you travel from your house to Washington, DC?
   ▶ In what ways might you be able to use Yahoo's search engine in your personal and school activities?

16. Exit your browser.

17. In your assigned team, discuss your findings from this activity, the importance of cartography, and how you may use this site in your school, home, and work activities.

Activity 20
Researching the Federal Reserve System

The federal government set up the **Federal Reserve System** (also known as the **Fed**) to supervise and regulate member banks in order to help the banks serve the public efficiently. Although state banks may choose to participate, all national banks are required to join the system. Those banks that join are known as **member banks**.

The United States is divided into twelve Federal Reserve districts each with a central Federal Reserve Bank. These Federal Reserve Banks are actually banks for banks. As an individual, you cannot open a savings account or borrow money from a Federal Reserve bank. The Fed serves only the member banks. Even so, the Federal Reserve affects all of us by its ability to control monetary policy. The Federal Reserve may lower interest rates, for example, to stimulate the economy. In turn, member banks lower the interest rate for their customers.

After you complete this activity, you will be able to:

- Explain the duties of the Federal Reserve System.
- Download a software program—Adobe Acrobat® Reader—from the Internet.
- Read documents from within Acrobat Reader while still connected to the Net.
- Determine which Federal Reserve bank is closest to you.
- Compose a report on the purposes and functions of the Federal Reserve System.

To learn more about the Federal Reserve System, let's explore the Internet.

1. Launch your browser to begin your exploration.

2. Go to the Federal Reserve web site at this URL:
   http://www.bog.frb.fed.us/
   Review the links provided on the Federal Reserve home page.

3. Link to the About the Federal Reserve System page.
   - ▶ When was the Federal Reserve System founded?
   - ▶ What are the four major duties of the Federal Reserve?

4. Go back to the Federal Reserve Board home page, and link to *Purposes and Functions*. Review the outline for *Purposes & Functions*, a publication of the Board of Governors of the Federal Reserve System.

   From this web page you can download the entire *Purposes & Functions* publication or selected chapters.

5. The *Purposes and Functions* publication is formatted for viewing with the Adobe Acrobat Reader software. If you don't have this program,

The *us* is an international top-level domain name for the United States.

PDF is an acronym for portable document format.

download the Acrobat Reader to your computer—*free of charge*. Link to <u>Obtaining the Acrobat Reader from the Adobe Web Site</u>, or enter the following URL: **http://www.adobe.com/acrobat/**
Your screen should be similar to the Adobe page in Figure 2-23.

Important: Check with your teacher to make sure that you should download the Acrobat Reader program to your computer from Adobe's web site. The download process may take 15–30 minutes or longer, depending on the speed of your Internet connection.

Follow the steps given at the Adobe site to download the appropriate version of the Acrobat Reader for your system. You must choose from among several operating systems (Windows, Macintosh, OS/2, UNIX, and so on) and languages (English, French, German, and so on). Once you download the program, you may have to complete the process by running the program to install the software on your computer.

Figure 2-23
Adobe Acrobat Page

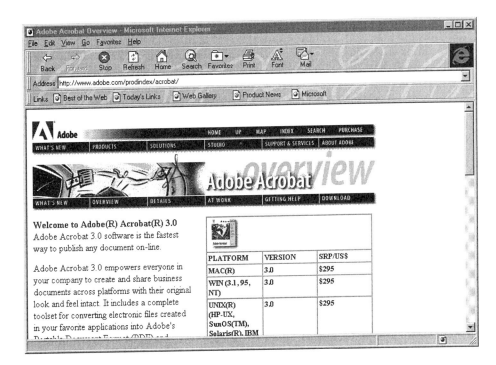

Use your browser to "go" directly to a previously viewed page.

6. Go back to the *Purposes and Functions* page. Download Chapter 1 – Overview of the Federal Reserve System. Choose to save the file to disk. Enter **OVERVIEW** as the file name when prompted.

7. Run the Acrobat Reader program, and open the OVERVIEW file. Scan the document to review its contents. You do not have to exit your browser to read the overview. If the text is too small to read, use the "magnify" option to increase the text display size.
   ▸ How can you order *Purposes & Functions*?
   ▸ How much does the publication cost if you order it?
   ▸ Why did Congress establish the Federal Reserve System?
   ▸ Which president signed the act?

8. *Optional:* Download several of the other chapters.

Important: Check with your teacher before you download any additional chapters.

9. Return to the Federal Reserve home page. Link to <u>Related Web Sites: Federal Reserve Banks</u>. Observe the locations of the twelve Federal Reserve banks. Most of the member bank sites have something similar to a "visitor's center" for you to visit, read, and learn more about the Federal Reserve System. Link to the Federal Reserve Bank site that is closest to where you live.

   ▶ What is the street address for the member bank's main office nearest where you live?

   ▶ Are there any branch offices in the district? If so, where are they located?

10. Exit your browser.

11. Using your word processing software, prepare a report that summarizes your findings about the Federal Reserve System. Some topics for discussion include the following:

   ▶ How was U.S. money distributed prior to the establishment of the Federal Reserve System in 1913?

   ▶ How is the Federal Reserve structured to affect monetary policy?

   ▶ Who are the members of the board of governors?

   ▶ How are the board members appointed?

   ▶ Who is the current Federal Reserve chairman?

   ▶ What makes the Federal Reserve independent within the government?

   ▶ Who makes monetary policy?

Activity 21
Finding Clip Art

"A picture is worth a thousand words." We've all heard this phrase. Do you prefer to read text that has interesting pictures associated with it? Most of us do! Would your documents be more interesting with pictures? Most of us agree that graphics enhance documents by visually enticing people to read what you have to say. But do you know where or how to get the pictures?

Adding graphics to a document, a newsletter, or a web page is as simple as purchasing clip art packages. You do not have to dig deep into your pockets, however, to acquire professional-quality graphics. Many are available from the Internet for no charge.

After you complete this activity, you will be able to:

- Explain the legal use of clip art obtained from the Internet.
- Search for subject area clip art.
- Understand the different types of graphic files.
- Save graphics to use in a document.
- Create a newsletter with clip art.

To learn more about finding clip art, let's explore the Internet.

1. Launch your browser to begin your exploration.

The top-level domain *net* identifies this site as a network service provider site.

2. Go to the The Clip Art Connection web site at this URL:
   http://www.acy.digex.net/~infomart/clipart
   This web site provides access to thousands of images that you can download and use in your documents. Your screen should be similar to The Clip Art Connection page in Figure 2-24 on page 80.

To learn more about copyrights, visit The Copyright Website! at URL: **http:// www.benedict.com/**

3. Link to <u>About Copyrights</u>, and read this topic.
   - ▶ Are you allowed to use clip art from these sites in your documents?
   - ▶ Can you sell the clip art you save or download from this site?
   - ▶ Does this policy apply to any graphics you see as you browse the Internet?

4. Go back to The Clip Art Connection home page. Find color clip art with an educational theme.
   Note: Link to <u>Theme Specific Clip Art</u>, <u>Education</u>, and then <u>Education-Related Color Clipart</u>. Depending on your Internet connection, you may have to wait several minutes to display some pages that contain a lot of graphics. At any time you can stop the transfer and then begin working with the images already appearing on your computer screen.

Remember that you sometimes have to scroll through information to see the entire page and the hypertext links you want.

5. A web site may include a variety of graphic or picture types. You can usually identify the type of graphic by the file name extension. Here are some typical extensions for graphics:

Figure 2-24
The Clip Art Connection
Page

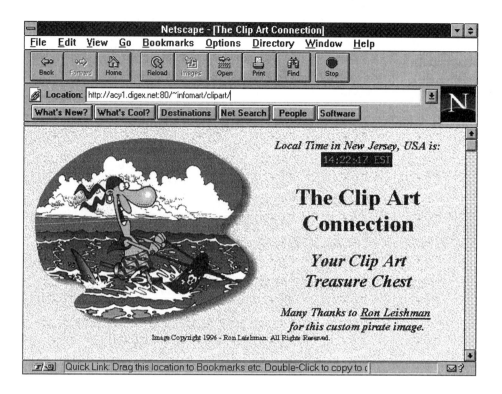

GIF	Commonly used format for images that appear on a web page.
PCX	An MS-DOS format used by many paint programs.
TIFF (or **TIF**)	Very complicated format with hundreds of options.
JPEG (or **JPG**)	Designed specifically to store digitized, full-color, or black-and-white photographs.
PICT	Commonly used format for images created using a Macintosh computer.
BMP	Not used much on the Net because BMP files tend to be very large.

Save any of the images at this site that interest you to a floppy disk or
your hard drive.

Note: If you are using Netscape Navigator or Microsoft Internet
Explorer on a Windows-compatible computer, position the mouse
pointer on an image and click the right mouse button. Choose the
appropriate option to save the image. Macintosh users should point to
a picture, click the mouse, and then choose to save the image. If you are
using a different browser, refer to the help or documentation to learn
how to save to disk an image that appears on a web page.

▶ What is the format of the images you just saved—GIF, JPEG, TIFF,
or PICT?

▶ Does your desktop publishing or paint software support the formats?

6. Go back to The Clip Art Connection home page. Scan through the
other areas and find one or two more graphics. Save the images to disk.

7. Exit your browser.

8. *Optional:* Print your favorite image.

9. In your assigned team, use your desktop publishing software to create a one-page newsletter that describes some of your favorite web sites. Use at least two clip art images in the newsletter.

Activity 22
Researching How to Dress for Success

Think about an instance when you were introduced to someone for the first time. What factors influenced your first impression of the individual? More than likely, the person's personality and outward appearance had an impact on your impression of the person.

The type of clothing we wear for various occasions often leaves lasting memories in others' minds. Casual attire is appropriate for some occasions, such as a sports event, a family gathering, or an outing with your friends. On the other hand, business attire is required for such occasions as a business meeting, a job interview, or an awards dinner. By now you probably know the importance of asking about appropriate dress for particular occasions so that you will feel comfortable and be able to perform your best. You should also remember that you have only one chance to make your first impression on others.

Do you know the dress code in any of the companies in your geographical area? In this activity you will conduct research to learn about dress codes. In today's business world, the dress code varies from business attire at all times to a mix of business attire on some days and casual attire on other days to casual attire every day. The definition of casual attire may also vary from one business to another. The dress code may be dependent on the type of work the employees do or the company's culture. Dress codes are also a topic of discussion in many publications.

After you complete this activity, you will be able to:

- Research information about dress codes in the business world.
- Find an e-mail address for several companies.
- Send an e-mail message to several businesses regarding their dress code.
- Read replies to your e-mail messages.
- Analyze the findings, and compose a report.

To learn about dress codes in businesses, let's explore the Internet.

1. Launch your browser to begin your exploration.

Searching for information takes time and patience.

2. Go to a search engine to find the name, street address, and e-mail addresses of three companies that interest you as a potential future employer. Here are the URLs for popular search engines:

AltaVista	**http://www.altavista.digital.com/**
Lycos	**http://www.lycos.com/**
Yahoo	**http://www.yahoo.com/**
Excite	**http://www.excite.com/**
Magellan	**http://www.mckinley.com/**

Note: Many web sites have an e-mail address on one of its pages.

> ▸ What are the names of the companies you are going to explore in this activity?
>
> ▸ What are their e-mail addresses?
>
> ▸ What are their street addresses?

3. Explore for several articles on dress codes in the business world.
   Note: Ask your teacher whether you may print articles or save them to disk for later reference.

   > ▸ From the articles you read, what conclusions can you make about dress codes?

Review the netiquette and e-mail information in the Introduction of this book.

4. Using your mail software, compose and send an e-mail message to each of the companies you located in order to learn about their dress code. Ask each company to describe its current dress code practices. Be sure to explain that you are conducting research for a school project and you would like a reply by a particular date. You may use the sample message in Figure 2-25 as a model.

Figure 2-25
Sample E-Mail Message Related to Dress Codes

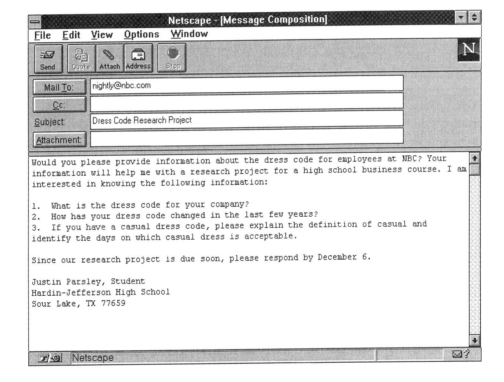

5. On a daily basis, check your e-mail software for a reply to your messages. When you receive a reply, print a copy of the message to use in team discussion.
   Note: Ask your teacher whether you may print your e-mail messages and whether you should file your messages or delete them.

6. Exit your browser.

7. In your assigned team, discuss the information you learned about dress codes in the business world, and share the replies you received from the companies. What conclusions can your team make about dress codes in the business world?

8. In your assigned team, use your word processing or desktop publishing software to compose a report on your findings about dress codes, and recommend ways you might be able to use this information to dress for success.

Activity 23
Serving Your Community

In today's world we hear much talk about people helping others. Community service shows support to individuals and to groups to make the world a better place. Examples of community organizations include parent-teacher organizations at schools, band and athletic boosters, city councils, park and recreation departments, literacy programs, and church-sponsored groups. You can use telecommunications to share ideas and to establish a network of people to exchange interests and support. As a result you may help your community in many ways.

Have you ever participated in a community organization as a volunteer? Many community-supported organizations need volunteers to help with their services and to communicate their services to others. As a volunteer for a community organization, you can be the "voice" of the organization to your friends and family. You can post announcements of community happenings, and you can participate in special events for the organization.

National organizations, such as the American Red Cross and the American Heart Association, can also benefit from your involvement. Volunteering for organizations such as these can provide an opportunity to contribute time and energy to the organization, to help others, and to prepare you for work in your community.

After you complete this activity, you will be able to:

- Search for information about community organizations.
- Identify a community service organization that interests you.
- Interview a representative from the community service organization.
- Compose an article about the community service organization.
- Post an article to a newsgroup.
- Identify the value and benefits of community organizations.

To learn about community service organizations, let's explore the Internet.

1. Launch your browser to begin your exploration.

2. Go to the American Red Cross web site at this URL:
   http://www.redcross.org/
   Your screen should be similar to the American Red Cross home page in Figure 2-26 on page 86. Explore various links to learn about the American Red Cross.
   ▶ What is the mission of the American Red Cross?
   ▶ What services does the American Red Cross offer?
   ▶ How can individuals help the American Red Cross?

   The top-level domain org identifies this site as an organization site.

3. Go to a search engine at one of these URLs:
   AltaVista   **http://www.altavista.digital.com/**
   Lycos   **http://www.lycos.com/**

Figure 2-26
American Red Cross
Home Page

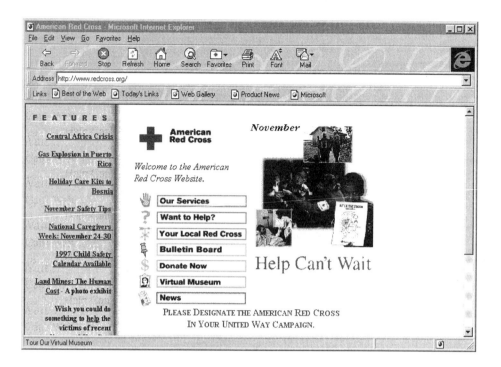

Yahoo	**http://www.yahoo.com/**
Excite	**http://www.excite.com/**
Magellan	**http://www.mckinley.com/**

4. Search for information about community organizations, their importance, and your role in serving your community.

5. Identify a list of local community service organizations, and choose one that interests you. You may want to go to the Yahoo home page at this URL: **http://www.yahoo.com/**

    Link to <u>U.S. States</u> and then to a state. Then continue choosing links to search for a list of community organizations in your city or a nearby community.

    Note: You may want to review the steps you followed in Activity 19 when you searched for a list of Internet service providers in your community.

    ▶ What is the name of a community service organization that interests you?

    ▶ What is the organization's address and phone number?

    ▶ What are the directions to the service organization?

6. Exit your browser.

7. Contact the service organization; explain that you are doing a school project and would like to interview a representative to learn more about the organization. During the interview, ask questions (and take notes) about the organization's history, mission, services provided, special events (dates, times, and location), volunteer program, youth involvement, and a contact person (name, address, phone, fax, and e-mail

address). Then discuss how you want to contribute to the organization by posting an article to a newsgroup about the community service organization.

Note: Realize that you may have to explain the value of telecommunications services in terms of communicating to the "world" about the community service organization. Inform the organization that you will share your article about the organization with them *before* you post it to the newsgroup. Be sure to ask who needs to approve the article.

8. Using your word processing software, compose an article that describes the community service organization you researched. Include appropriate information to emphasize the importance of the organization and how to become involved. Save and print the file.

Proofread to correct all spelling, punctuation, and grammar errors.

9. Ask a classmate to proofread your article and offer constructive criticism. Then make the necessary revisions to your article.

10. Share the final version of the article with your teacher for feedback *before* you communicate with the organization.

11. Share the article with the organization for their approval. Also identify to the organization the newsgroup to which you will post the article.

Remember that all members of the newsgroup will receive a copy of the article. Review the newsgroup information in the Introduction.

12. Launch your browser, and open your newsreader.

13. Compose your e-mail message. Remember to open your article. Then post the article to a newsgroup.

    Note: Your teacher will tell you to which newsgroup to post the article.

14. Print your posting, and exit your newsreader. Then exit your browser.

15. In your assigned team, discuss the value of community organizations and the personal benefits of involvement. Share your related community organization experiences. How will you use your new knowledge of community organizations to serve your community?

Activity 24
Defining Your Community

Have you always lived in the same community, or have you moved from one location to another at least one time? What do you enjoy about your community? How does your community influence your daily attitude?

In today's fast-paced world, career changes and job opportunities, family health concerns, and special interests are the leading reasons you may have to move from one location to another. Sometimes the adjustment to a new location is fairly short and relatively painless. At other times the adjustment to a new location may be terribly difficult. You may have to leave friends and family far behind. The climate might be totally different from that of your current hometown. You may move from a rural area with very little traffic and noise to an area with heavy traffic, air pollution, and a higher crime rate.

What do you and others know about your community or a community you like? What makes your community so special? The Internet offers much information about communities. And some of the information related to details about annual weather, travel, events, census bureau statistics, and education you would not be able to find in the local newspapers. In addition, you can secure information about a community via telecommunications.

After you complete this activity, you will be able to:

- Search for information about a community that interests you.
- Compose a questionnaire.
- Send the questionnaire to a listserv.
- Read the replies to your e-mail message.
- Analyze your findings and compose a report.

To learn about a community, let's explore the Internet.

1. Launch your browser to begin your exploration.

Searching for information takes time and patience.

2. Go to a search engine to explore for information about a community where you might someday want to live. Search for specific information to learn all you can about the chosen community. You may want to explore for information related to the chamber of commerce, education, businesses, entertainment, health facilities, churches, and cultural information.
   Note: You may want to review the steps you followed in Activity 19 and Activity 23 to narrow your search for specific information. As you conduct research, record appropriate information to use in your report at the end of this activity. You may also want to ask your teacher whether you may print articles or save them to disk for later reference.

   Consider these or other search engines:

   | AltaVista | **http://www.altavista.digital.com/** |
   | Lycos | **http://www.lycos.com/** |

Yahoo   http://www.yahoo.com/
Excite   http://www.excite.com/
Magellan   http://www.mckinley.com/

Scroll down an entire page to see the hyper- text links you may want to explore.

3. Go to The Weather Channel web site at this URL: **http://www.weather.com/** to explore various links to find weather information for your chosen community.

4. Go to the U.S. Census Bureau web site at this URL: **http://www.census.gov/** to explore various links to find statistical information about your chosen community.
   Note: You can search the Census Bureau site by words, places, and maps.

5. Go to The National Park Service ParkNet web site at this URL: **http://www.nps.gov/** to explore for recreational information about your chosen community.

6. Exit your browser.

Refer to the Introduc- tion for information on listservs.

7. To gain additional information about the community you chose, let's send a questionnaire to a listserv. Using your word processing software, compose a questionnaire. You may refer to the model in Figure 2-27 as you compose your questionnaire.

Figure 2-27
Sample Questionnaire
Related to Community

Would you please take a few minutes to complete this short question- naire about your community? As a school project for my high school class, I am gathering information to see whether I would like to move to your community someday. Please send your replies to my e-mail address [*insert your e-mail address*] by [*insert date*]. Use COMMUNITY–[*insert your name*] as the subject of your reply.

1. Describe the typical weather during the four seasons of the year.

2. Identify the primary features of your community.

3. If you had the time and money to spend, what two things would you do to improve your community? Why?

4. Identify these facts about your community:
   City:
   State:
   Zip:
   Area Code:
   Estimated Population:

5. If you provide the following information, you can expect to receive a report of my findings by [*insert date*].
   Name:
   Age:
   Work or School Name:
   Your E-mail Address:

   [*Type your name, school, city and state, and your e-mail address*]

8. Proofread and edit the questionnaire. Also ask a classmate to proofread your questionnaire.
   Note: Be sure to save your text file with a file name less than eight characters.

9. Start your e-mail software.

10. Compose a mail message. Remember to copy your questionnaire file as the body of your mail message. Then post the questionnaire you created to this listserv: IECC–Projects.
    Note: The IECC–Projects listserv helps students communicate with international and intercultural classes through e-mail projects. To subscribe and unsubscribe to this list, send an e-mail message to iecc-projects-request@stolaf.edu

11. Exit your e-mail software and your browser.

12. On a daily basis, check your e-mail messages for replies to your questionnaire. Remember to look for mail with COMMUNITY–[*your name*] as the subject. Print the replies you receive.
    Note: Ask your teacher whether you should file your replies or delete them.

13. Using your word processing or desktop publishing software, compose a report of your findings about the community you researched. Include information from your research on the Internet and from the responses you received. Based on your findings, evaluate whether you would enjoy moving to the community. Follow the style for a typical report format by including a title page, table of contents, header or footer, headings, and at least one graphic.

Activity 25
Planning for a Career

Have you decided what you want to be when you "grow up"? Have you studied any career information to know the types of occupations within your career choice, the positions, the educational requirements, and the expected wages? Do you know the advantages and disadvantages of a chosen occupation? Do you know whether your interests and aptitudes match the particular field?

In today's world you have numerous career options. The path your life takes depends heavily on one critical factor: planning. **Career planning** is the process of studying a career, assessing your strengths and weaknessses in terms of the career and occupations within the career, setting goals, and then making decisions to reach your goals. You can learn about careers and educational requirements from guidance counselors; teachers; school organizations such as Junior Achievement, Future Business Leaders of America, and Business Professionals of America; books; and researching on the Internet.

After you complete this activity, you will be able to:

- Use a search engine to search the Internet for career information.
- Search for a newsgroup related to your chosen career and occupation.
- Research newsgroup articles.
- Analyze your personality test results as related to your chosen career.
- Compose a report about your career findings.

To learn about a particular career, let's explore the Internet.

1. Decide which career and occupation you want to explore.
   - ▶ What career do you want to study?
   - ▶ In what occupational area do you have an interest?

2. In your assigned team, identify a list of questions related to careers that you would like to explore on the Internet. Consider searching for information related to occupations, educational requirements, job responsibilities, geographic locations, compensation, benefits, and so on.

3. Launch your browser to begin your exploration.

4. Go to the Magellan (a search engine) web site at this URL:
   http://www.mckinley.com/
   Search the Internet for information related to your chosen career and occupation by linking first to <u>Employment</u> and then to the career area. Explore various links to find related articles.
   Note: As you conduct research, take appropriate notes or print articles or save them to disk for later reference.
   - ▶ What keywords did you use to explore for related information?
   - ▶ How successful was your search for information on the Internet?

The content and links on a web page may change at any time. Explore the page to find links that match your search critteria.

5. Now let's search for a newsgroup that relates to your chosen career area. Go to the Deja News Research Service web site at this URL: **http://www.dejanews.com/**
Deja News Research Service is a tool for searching through thousands of postings in thousands of newsgroups. Deja News is free and easy to use.

6. Link to <u>Newsgroups</u>. Scroll through the information on this page, and link to <u>Using Deja News to find what you want</u>. Read about the various ways to search for articles and newsgroups.

7. Link to <u>Ask DN Wizard</u> to review the FAQs at this site.

8. Go back to the Using Deja News to find what you want page, and link to <u>Query Profile</u>. Your screen should be similar to Figure 2-28. This page will allow you to search for newsgroups. In the Easy Query Profile Form, type the topic you want to search for: **job** or **career**. Then process your search request.
Note: When you are searching for a newsgroup, you should first try broad keywords. Based on the search results, narrow your search with more specific keywords.

Figure 2-28
Deja News Easy Query Profile Form Page

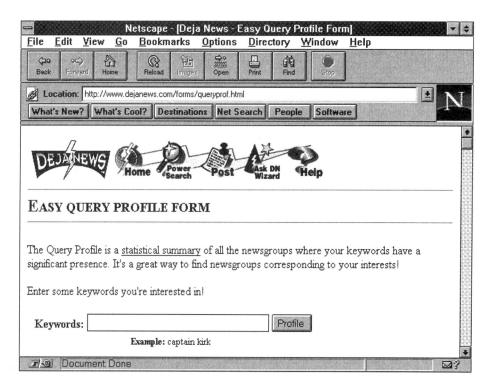

9. A Query Profile will list the newsgroups in which your keyword most often appears. Check the newsgroups to include in the filter, and create the filter.

10. Note the results of your search on the Filtered Power Search page. In the appropriate field, type your chosen career or occupation to narrow or limit the search. Then select additional search options, and process the search request.

11. After a few moments a list of the specific articles that meet your search requirements will appear on your screen. Read some of the articles in selected newsgroups to determine whether a particular newsgroup contains related information. Continue searching for several newsgroups related to your career.

    Note: You may link from one article to the next. Be sure to record the name of any interesting newsgroups in your journal.

    ▶ What are the names of several newsgroups that relate to your chosen career?

12. Go directly to the newsgroups you identified in your search. Explore various articles until you have sufficient research information to answer your questions about the particular career area. Then exit the newsgroups.

    Note: Subscribing to a newsgroup is free. Access online help to review the steps to subscribe and unsubscribe to a newsgroup.

    ▶ What information relates to your career?

Ask your teacher for permission to subscribe to a newsgroup.

13. *Optional:* Compose an article to send to a newsgroup to ask specific questions related to your chosen career and occupation.

    Note: Ask your teacher whether you should complete this step. If you are assigned this step, ask your teacher to approve your article before you send it.

14. Exit your browser.

15. Review your personality test results in Activity 16—Evaluating Your Personality.

    ▶ How does your personality type match the requirements for your chosen career?

16. Using your word processing or desktop publishing software, compose a report that includes a summary of your findings, your recommendations, occupational areas, educational requirements, expected salary, and potential job outlook. How will you use the information you learned in this activity?

Activity 26
Preparing Your Résumé

In Activity 25 you explored information to help you plan for a career. You also evaluated your personality as it relates to your career choice. At some point in your life, you will be ready to search for a job—perhaps in the career area you have just studied. When that time comes, you will undoubtedly need to prepare a résumé. Do you know the purpose of a résumé? Do you know the types of information to include in a résumé?

> A résumé is a unique presentation of who you are. No two résumés are identical.

A **résumé** is a one- or two-page summary that identifies your strengths, education, experience, and skills. Basically a résumé says who you are, what you have learned, and what you have accomplished. As you prepare a résumé, remember to present relevant, honest information to result in achieving one primary purpose: to get a job interview. Your résumé, therefore, must create a positive first impression. Then during the interview you can further discuss the ways in which you can contribute to the particular company.

In today's world, job searches are not limited to the traditional job leads: talking with others or networking, analyzing ads, and working with job placement firms. The Internet has a wealth of information related to employment, résumé preparation, and interviewing. In addition, the Internet offers another medium to share your résumé with the world. By developing an HTML document, you can post your résumé online.

After you complete this activity, you will be able to:

- Search for information on résumé preparation.
- Compose a résumé.
- Identify the steps to create an HTML document.
- Prepare an HTML document.
- Discuss the value of a well-written résumé and an HTML document.

To prepare a résumé and an HTML document, let's explore the Internet.

1. Launch your browser to begin your exploration.

2. Go to the JobWeb home page at this URL: **http://www.jobweb.org/** Your screen should be similar to Figure 2-29 on page 95. Note the links on this page, and link to Career Planning Resources.

3. Now link to Job Search and then to The Résumé. Explore all the links related to information about résumés.

   ▸ What is a résumé?
   ▸ What is the purpose of a résumé?
   ▸ Identify the parts of a résumé.
   ▸ What type of résumé format should you follow?
   ▸ How long should your résumé be?
   ▸ Should you ask others to critique your résumé?

Figure 2-29
JobWeb Home Page

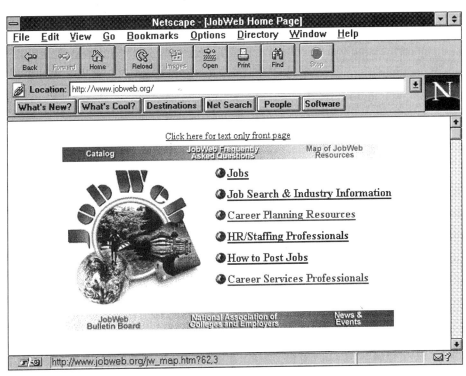

JobWeb is a trademark of the National Association of Colleges and Employers.

> ▶ What factors should you consider to enhance the "scan-ability" of your résumé?
> ▶ How can you place your résumé online?

4. Go to your favorite search engine site, and perform a search of online résumés. Explore various sites to see others' résumés.
   Note: As you explore you may want to make notes regarding formats and content styles that get your attention. You may also want to ask your teacher whether you can print or save to disk related information.

5. Exit your browser.

6. Using your word processing software, compose your résumé.
   Note: Remember to include all the critical information that best represents who you are and what you have to offer a company.

Remember that your résumé must never have any grammar or spelling errors.

7. Exchange your résumé with a classmate. Critique each other's work, and offer constructive criticism.

8. Ask a friend, parent, or teacher to critique your résumé for feedback related to the appearance and content.
   Note: Thoughtfully consider the feedback you receive. Revise your résumé, as appropriate.

HTML stands for hyper-text markup language.

9. Let's assume you want to place your résumé online. To do so, you must use correct HTML format. Launch your browser again.

10. Go to the A Beginner's Guide to HTML page at this URL:
    http://www.ncsa.uiuc.edu/General/Internet/WWW/ HTMLPrimer.html
    Your screen should be similar to Figure 2-30 on page 96. A Beginner's

Figure 2-30
A Beginner's Guide to
HTML Page

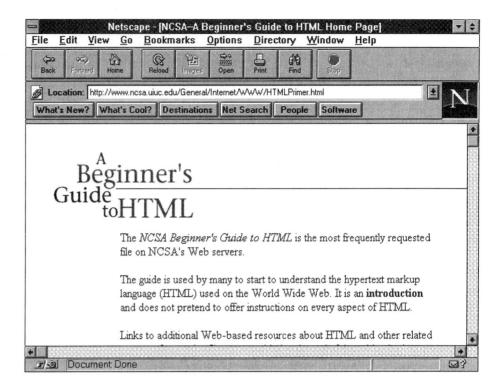

Guide to HTML provides an introduction to using HTML and step-by-step instructions to create an HTML document. Scroll through the outline of the content of Parts 1, 2, and 3. Then explore numerous links, beginning with Getting Started, to learn how to create an HTML document.

▸ What is the difference between *HTML* and *SGML*?

▸ Identify several elements in an HTML document?

▸ What is an HTML tag?

▸ How can you see the copy of the file your browser reads to generate a web page?

▸ How can you go about placing an HTML document on a server?

▸ How do you include links in an HTML document?

Carefully follow the steps to prepare an HTML document.

11. With an assigned team member, prepare an HTML version of your résumé and your team member's résumé.
Note: As you work together, help each other access and apply the appropriate material at the A Beginner's Guide to HTML page.

12. *Optional:* Post your résumé to an online résumé site.

13. In an assigned team, share your résumés with each other. Evaluate the various styles in terms of content and appearance. Discuss how you will apply the new knowledge and skills you learned in this activity in your personal lives.

Activity 27
Advertising on the WWW

Before the World Wide Web, many companies advertised their merchandise and services using "traditional" advertising media. Newspaper advertisements, television commercials, brochures, and billboards were some of the ways companies informed consumers and persuaded them to buy their products.

As more and more people "surf the Net," the Internet has become an important place for businesses to reach consumers. Billboards, which once appeared exclusively along our roads and interstate highways, now appear everywhere on the information superhighway. Almost every web site you visit will have one or more advertisements.

Unlike traditional print media, the Internet offers businesses a dynamic way to present their products. Advertising on the web varies from simple buttons to animated messages. And given the interactive nature of the Internet, a consumer can link to a company's web page to learn more about a product. At some sites a consumer can even purchase products.

After you complete this activity, you will be able to:

- Identify different kinds of advertising on the Internet.
- List common placement of advertising on a web page.
- Link to another site from an advertisement.
- Compare and contrast Internet advertising.
- Design an advertisement for the Internet.

To learn more about advertising on the web, let's explore the Internet.

1. Launch your browser.
   Note: Most advertisements that appear on the Internet are best viewed using a graphical browser. If you are using a text-based browser, you will not be able to see the advertisements.

Advertisements provide a significant source of revenue for those companies that own and operate the search engine web sites.

2. Many of the search engines include advertisements. Go to any one of the search engine sites listed below.

AltaVista	**http://www.altavista.digital.com/**
Excite	**http://www.excite.com/**
Lycos	**http://www.lycos.com/**
Magellan	**http://www.mckinley.com/**
Yahoo	**http://www.yahoo.com/**

   ▶ Do any advertisements appear on the home page? If so, what are they?

Most browsers support animated pictures and images to draw attention to an advertisement.

3. Use the search engine to find information on advertisements. Type **advertisements** as the keyword.

   ▶ Are there any advertisements on the search results page?

> ▸ Are the advertisements animated?
>
> ▸ Describe how animation is used in the advertisement.
>
> ▸ Where are the advertisements located on the web page—top, bottom, or side?

4. From the search web site, link to "cool sites" or "top 5% sites" to locate a list of popular web sites.
   Note: If you are using Netscape Navigator, click the **What's Cool** directory button for a list of new sites. Microsoft Internet Explorer users can click the **Today's Links** button.

5. Choose a site that interests you. Link to and explore the site. Notice if there are any advertisements on the web pages.

   > ▸ List the products and services advertised.
   >
   > ▸ Record the advertisers, specials, prices, and special eye-catching features.
   >
   > ▸ Identify the location of each advertisement as it appears on a web page.

6. Repeat step 5 to explore at least three web sites.

7. Go to the *USA Today* home page at this URL:
   http://www.usatoday.com
   This site is based on the popular *USA Today* newspaper. Much of the content is re-purposed for the interactive environment found on the Internet. Explore the web site. (See Figure 2-31.)

   > ▸ Record the advertisements that appear throughout this online publication.
   >
   > ▸ List the products and services featured in the advertisements.

Remember that many graphical browsers let you save a file containing an image from a web page. Position the pointer on an image, click (or right-click) the mouse button, and choose to save the image.

Figure 2-31
USA Today Money Page

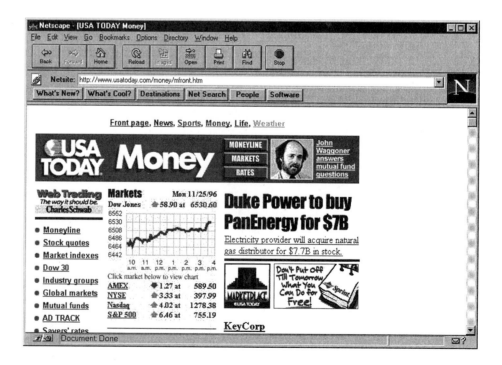

Many advertisements contain links to other web sites.

8. After exploring the *USA Today* web site, find an advertisement that contains a link to the company sponsoring the advertisement. Then link to the company to learn more about the advertised product. Record information about the product in the advertisement.

9. Go back to the *same* search engine you explored earlier in this activity. Perform another search by typing **advertisements** as the keyword again. Note the advertisement that appears on the search results page.

   ▶ Does the same advertisement as shown last time appear?

   Unlike traditional print media that is static, many web sites present different advertisements every few minutes. If you performed another search now, the search results page could display a completely different advertisement. Some web sites even use information sent by your browser to customize an advertisement.

10. Exit your browser.

11. Using your word processing or desktop publishing software, summarize the results of your findings.

    ▶ What kinds of products are advertised on the web?
    ▶ What techniques are used to emphasize the advertisements?
    ▶ How do the Internet advertisements compare to more traditional forms of advertising?
    ▶ Explain how online advertisements differ from television commercials, newspaper advertisements, and other similar media.

12. Using your paint program or illustration software, design an online advertisement that will promote an upcoming event at your school. Keep in mind the placement on the page (screen), size of the advertisements and the graphics, font styles and sizes, colors, and other factors you saw while working through this activity.

Activity 28
Comparing Phone Rates

Local telephone companies provide a variety of communication services to homes, schools, and businesses. With the growing popularity of the Internet, demand for certain kinds of services, such as high-speed telephone connections, is increasing rapidly. As the use of graphics, animation, audio, and video increases on the World Wide Web, so does the need for higher bandwidth.

During the past few years legislation has passed to provide consumers with more affordable rates for these high-speed connections and other basic telephone services. However, deregulation has resulted in many other changes that will affect all consumers. For example, cable television operators are now permitted to offer telephone services. And local and long-distance telephone carriers can expand into each other's markets.

How will these changes affect you? Will you pay higher or lower rates for telephone services? What new telephone options are available? Using the Internet, you can gather information about the variety of telephone services available.

After you complete this activity, you will be able to:

- Identify the rates and features for services provided by your local telephone company.
- Compare the rates and services offered by long-distance carriers.
- Compose a report about telephone services.
- Create a spreadsheet that compares telephone rates.

To learn about telephone services and phone rates, let's explore the Internet.

1. Launch your browser to begin your exploration.

2. Determine whether your local telephone company has a web site. Use a search engine, such as Yahoo, to locate this information.

   A partial list of web sites for local telephone service providers is given below. Use one of these sites if you cannot locate a web site for your telephone company.

   Bell Atlantic   http://www.BellAtlantic.com/
   Bell South   http://www.bellsouth.com/
   Cincinnati Bell   http://www.CinBellTel.com/
   Southwestern Bell   http://www.sbc.com/
   US West   http://www.uswest.com/

3. Go to the home page of your local telephone service provider. (See Figure 2-32 on page 101.) Research the following topics.
   Note: Record the questions for which you cannot find information online. In step 6, you will prepare a brief questionnaire to obtain the remaining information off-line.

Use regional bell operating companies as the search keyword to help find a list of local telephone service providers.

Figure 2-32
Bell Atlantic Home Page

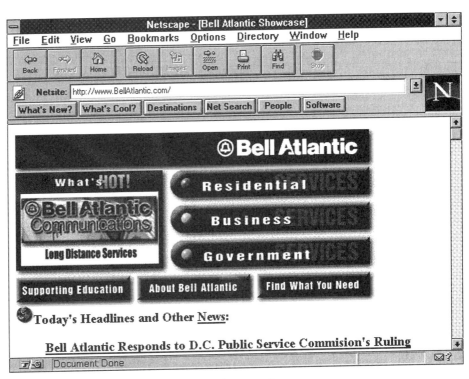

> ► What is the monthly rate for a plain old telephone service (POTS) residential phone line?
> ► Are any discounts available for multiple residential telephone lines?
> ► What are the monthly costs for special features such as call waiting, call forwarding, and caller identification?
> ► What is the monthly rate for a POTS business phone line?
> ► How much does the local phone company charge per month for an integrated services digital network (ISDN) line?
> ► What is the monthly rate for a T1 line?
> ► Does your local telephone company offer fiber optics service?
> ► Does your local telephone company offer long-distance service?

4. Contact at least three different long-distance carriers. Gather information regarding residential and business services. The URL addresses for a few of the more popular long-distance carriers are given below. Go to the URLs listed, or access a search engine to find other resources. (See Figure 2-33 on page 102.)

AT&T   **http://www.att.com/**
MCI   **http://www.mci.com/**
Sprint   **http://www.sprint.com/**

> ► What is the per minute rate (if available) for residential customers?
> ► Are special promotions available?
> ► Do businesses pay the same rate as residential customers for long-distance service?
> ► What is the per minute rate for a business that averages slightly less than $100 per month in long-distance charges?

Figure 2-33
AT&T Home Page

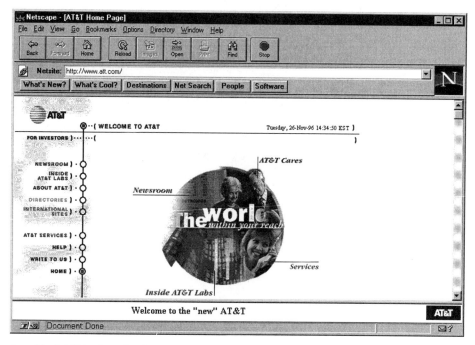

> ▶ What is the rate if a business averages about $500 per month in long-distance charges?
> ▶ What kinds of services do the long-distance carriers offer?

5. Exit your browser.

Be sure to ask your teacher's permission before calling. Whenever possible, use an 800 or 888 number to call toll free.

6. In your assigned team, prepare a questionnaire to gather any information you were unable to obtain online in steps 3 and 4. Either e-mail the questionnaire to your local telephone company and long-distance carriers, or call the customer service departments at the various companies.

7. Using your spreadsheet software, prepare a spreadsheet that compares the per minute rates for the three long-distance carriers. Show the rate information for two different levels—$100 per month and $500 per month.

8. Using your word processing or desktop publishing software, compose a report that summarizes the information you gathered about the telephone companies.

Activity 29
Exploring Project Gutenberg

Project Gutenberg is an ongoing effort to convert books, references, short stories, plays, poems, and other literary works into **electronic texts** (or **etexts**). Works by many renowned authors such as Nathaniel Hawthorne, Lucy Montgomery, William Shakespeare, and Mark Twain are part of this electronic collection. The project gets its name from Johann Gutenberg who invented one of the first modern printing presses in 1450.

As you learned in Activity 21, authors and publishers are granted a copyright for their works. During a set period, only those who hold the copyright may reproduce the materials. However, once a copyright expires (usually fifty or more years after the death of an author), the books become part of the public domain. Only then are these publications available to the general public to be copied or used for other purposes such as Project Gutenberg.

The etexts provided as part of Project Gutenberg are not stored in one central location. Rather, many individuals participate in this project and make the etexts available at numerous sites across the Internet. A master index and hypertext links from other sites allow easy access to your favorite classic.

After you complete this activity, you will be able to:

- Explain the purpose of Project Gutenberg.
- List some of the materials available from Project Gutenberg.
- Locate a book, poem, short story, or play of your choice.
- Download and read a file using the FTP protocol.
- Compose a summary of an etext.

To learn more about Project Gutenberg, let's explore the Internet.

1. Launch your browser to begin your exploration.

2. Go to the Project Gutenberg web site at this URL:
   http://www.promo.net/pg/
   Your screen should be similar to the Project Gutenberg page in Figure 2-34 on page 104. Review the links on this page.

3. Link to the page that describes Project Gutenberg.
   Optional: If you know German or are studying the language now, you may want to read the introduction in German.
   - ▶ Who founded Project Gutenberg and why?
   - ▶ How are the electronic texts (or etexts) distributed?

4. Go back to the home page, and then link to <u>Recent Releases</u>.
   - ▶ When was this list last updated?
   - ▶ What site provides up-to-the-minute releases?
   - ▶ List the titles of five recently released works.

The top-level domain *net* identifies the Project Gutenberg page as a page at a network provider site.

Figure 2-34
Project Gutenberg Page

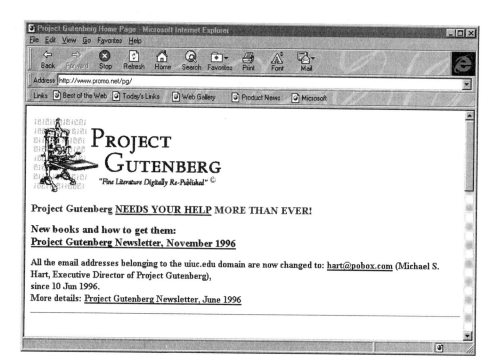

Remember that you can use the Find option to search for information on a page.

Project Gutenberg provides access to hundreds of literary works stored across the Internet.

5. Go back to the home page. Link to <u>Author and Title Listings</u>, and then go to the author listings.

   ▶ Who wrote *A Tale of Two Cities*?
   ▶ List three works published by Samuel Langhorne Clemens.
   ▶ Samuel Langhorne Clemens is more commonly known as whom?
   ▶ What titles did Nathaniel Hawthorne write?

6. Find your favorite classic in the list, or choose *The House of Seven Gables* if you can't decide. Link to the index page. You may have to wait a few minutes for your browser to go to the hypertext link you choose.

   If you have a graphical browser, you should see three sets of icons. Two icons are linked to each site of the three FTP download sites. The document icon links to a copy of the etext that you can download and immediately read using your browser. The other icon links to a compressed or "zipped" file. Although compressed files are faster to download, you need special software to uncompress them before you can read the etext.

   If you have a text browser, you should see six links (<u>1/Z 2/Z 3/Z</u>) after each title. These links represent the three FTP sites from which you can download etexts. At each site, you can download a text version (e.g., <u>1</u>) or a compressed (zipped) file (e.g., <u>Z</u>). Unless you have software to uncompress a file, you should download the text version.

7. Download the etext. It really does not matter from which site you choose to download the file, but you should not choose a compressed file unless you have the software needed to uncompress the file.

   If you download a text version, save the etext to your hard disk or a floppy disk to read later. You can use your browser or a word processor to read the etext.

   If you download a compressed file, specify a file name and a location.

Important: Check with your teacher to make sure that you should download an etext to your computer. The download process can take 15–30 minutes or longer, depending on the speed of your Internet connection.

Note: If you have difficulty downloading an etext, you can go directly to a Gutenberg FTP site such as **ftp://uiarchive.cso.uiuc.edu/pub/ etext/gutenberg/**
From there you can link to or download an index to help you locate where a particular etext is stored. Then link to that page and download the file.

8. Exit your browser.

9. Read the etext or a few chapters that you downloaded. Using your word processing software, prepare a short summary of the etext.
    Note: If you downloaded a compressed file, uncompress the etext file. Since the steps to uncompress a file depend on your operating system, ask your teacher for help with this process.

Activity 30
Investigating Computer Network Hardware

What do you need to connect computers to other computers? Wires, cables, telephone lines, modems, transceivers, Ethernet cards, hubs, and routers are important parts of the network communications systems needed to connect computers. To learn more about network communications, you will need to do some research.

One of the easiest ways to gather information and learn about the most up-to-date networking terminology is through the Internet. Some sources include online computer magazine articles and advertisements, research papers, and hardware manufacturers' web sites.

After you complete this activity, you will be able to:

- Locate resources to explore network communications topics.
- Define and use common network terminology.
- Identify the components necessary to connect computers to a network.
- Use off-line reference materials as additional resources.
- Prepare a cost comparison spreadsheet.
- Compose a report.

To learn about computer networking hardware, let's explore the Internet.

1. Launch your browser.

2. Go to the 3Com web site at this URL: **http://www.3com.com**
   Your screen should be similar to 3Com's home page shown in Figure 2-35 on page 107. Since 3Com manufactures various kinds of network hardware, this is a good place to begin your research.

3. Link to the <u>Networking Solutions Center</u>, and then link to <u>Glossary of Networking Terms</u>. Locate and review the definitions for the following terms:

ATM	hub	TCP/IP
bandwidth	ISDN	T1
Ethernet	router	WAN

4. Go back to the Networking Solutions Center page, and link to <u>Brochures</u>. Research information about ISDN modems.
   Note: Link to topics that include ISDN, Internet, connection, or other similar keywords.

   ▶ What is an ISDN modem?
   ▶ Does 3Com offer an ISDN modem?
   ▶ What are the features and specifications?
   ▶ How much does it cost?

You can save a page or copy/paste text from a web page into another document for later reference.

Remember to always follow the copyright guidelines.

If there are terms you do not recognize, link to the glossary for definitions.

Figure 2-35
3Com Home Page

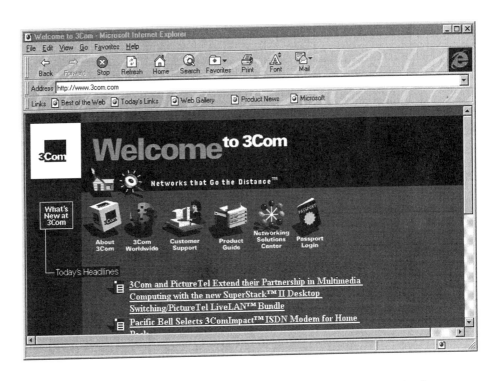

▶ What advantages does an ISDN modem offer over a standard modem?

▶ Can you connect an ISDN modem to a standard telephone line?

5. Search the Internet for other manufacturers that offer an ISDN modem. You may want to try these resources or use a search engine.

Bay Networks (network hardware manufacturer) at
   http://www.baynetworks.com/

Cisco Systems (network hardware manufacturer) at
   http://www.cisco.com/

Novell (network software provider) at **http://www.novell.com/**

Internet World (technology magazine) at **http://www.iw.com/**

PC Week Online (technology magazine) at **http://www.pcweek.com/**

▶ Do other manufacturers offer ISDN modems?

▶ Are the prices comparable?

▶ Do any of ISDN modems have different features?

Use your favorite search engine to locate additional resources.

6. Use the resources you learned about in this activity to research the following network topics.

▶ What hardware and software are required to set up a small local area network?

▶ What type of cabling or wiring is used to connect computers in a local area network?

▶ Is additional hardware required to connect to the World Wide Web?

▶ Can the Internet be used for video conferencing?

▶ What kind of hardware and software are required for video conferencing?

▶ What types of hardware is available for high-speed transmission?

7. Exit your browser.

8. Continue your research off-line to gather more information on ISDN modems and other network hardware/software. Ask your teacher, computer lab manager, administrator, librarian, or a local computer store manager for at least one computer catalog. Use the catalogs to find product and pricing information for a variety of network hardware and software products.

9. Using your spreadsheet software, prepare a cost comparison spreadsheet for similar network hardware products.

10. Using your word processing or desktop publishing software, compose a report that explains the hardware and software needed to set up a network. Be sure to define any technical terms. Provide cost figures, if available.

▶ **Part**

One Two Three

123

Glossary

Glossary

A

Acceptable Use Policy
AUP; a written contract between a school, a student, and the student's parents or guardian that identifies the rules and guidelines for using the Internet.

Address
See *E-mail address.*

Anonymous FTP
A service provided on some computers that lets you connect to certain remote computers and download files from large databases and archive sites without being a registered user. You generally must use the password *guest* or *anonymous.* (See *FTP.*)

ARPANET
An early network of computer networks funded by the United States Department of Defense Advanced Research Projects Agency (ARPA); the predecessor of the Internet.

ASCII
American Standard Code for Information Interchange; a collection of public domain character sets considered standard throughout the computer industry.

B

Bits per Second
bps; a measurement of telecommunications speed.

Bookmark
A feature of a browser that flags the location of a document. (See *Browser* and *Hot List.*)

Browser
A special software program required to navigate the World Wide Web that allows you to access information on the Internet. (See *Graphical Browser* and *Text Browser.*)

Bulletin Board System
BBS; a central computer used by special interest groups to exchange information on a particular topic. You can connect to a BBS through a phone line, your own computer, and a modem. Most BBSs offer files, programs, and other information that you can download to your own computer; some enable you to send e-mail and chat with other users who are connected at the same time.

C

Client
A term used to describe a computer connected to the Internet that has the capability to share information on the Internet.

com
A top-level domain that means commercial service. (See *Domain Extension.*)

Compressed Files
The format of many files on the Internet. Compressed files use less space than the original files and take less time to download than uncompressed files. To use a compressed file, you must first uncompress it via a special program.

Cyberspace
A term that means the electronic world of the Internet or the World Wide Web. (See *Information Superhighway.*)

D

Dedicated Internet Connection
A connection to the Internet that is active all the time through a permanent link to another Internet service provider.

Dial-up Internet Connection
A connection to the Internet that is active only while you are connected to an Internet service provider through your own computer and modem over a phone line.

Domain
The part of an Internet e-mail address after the @ symbol that identifies the computer where the user is working. For example, in billg@microsoft.com, *microsoft.com* is the domain. (See *Domain Name System,*

E-Mail Address, *Subdomain*, and *Username*.)

Domain Extension
Also called the **top-level domain**; the last three letters of an Internet address. Common domain extensions are *.com* for commercial service, *.edu* for education, *.gov* for government, *.mil* for military, *.net* for network provider, and *.org* for organization. A geographical top-level domain identifies a country on the Internet. For example, *us* represents United States, *at* represents Australia, and *ca* represents Canada.

Domain Name System
DNS; the system used to identify Internet addresses. An Internet address consists of a username and domain. (See *Domain*, *Domain Extension*, *E-Mail Address*, and *Username*.)

Download
To copy information or a file from a remote computer to a location on the user's local computer. (See *Upload*.)

E

Electronic Mail
Also called **e-mail**; the transfer of information from one computer to another in electronic format. Users can send text-based messages as well as multimedia documents. Typically, e-mail messages are stored safely in the recipient's electronic "mailbox" until the recipient reads them. Thus, the sender and the recipient need not be using the Internet at the same time.

E-Mail Address
A unique address that identifies you when you are connected to the Internet. Your e-mail address allows you to access information, and others may send information to your address. An e-mail address may be numeric, alphabetic, or a combination of numbers and letters. E-mail addresses always use lowercase letters with no spaces.

E-Mail Manager
Also called **mail reader**; a tool to manage e-mail and to communicate on the Internet. E-mail managers may be built into the communications software you are using. Your e-mail manager allows you to compose, read, reply, print, save, and delete mail messages.

Emoticons
A combination of symbols and letters usually sent with electronic mail that when combined display a little picture that expresses an emotion when you tilt your head to the left side. The most popular emoticon is the smiley, :-).

Encryption
Encoding sensitive information so that if it's intercepted a user without the proper key won't be able to understand it.

F

FAQ
Frequently Asked Question; refers to a page containing common questions about Internet services and their answers. This prevents individuals, newsgroup providers, and mailing list providers from having to answer the same questions repeatedly. Always check the FAQ list before you post a question.

Favorites
A term used by the browser Microsoft Internet Explorer to flag the location of a document. (See *Bookmark*.)

File Extension
A suffix to a file name that further identifies the contents of the file. For example, DOG.GIF indicates that this is a graphic file. Other common file name extensions for graphics include .PCX, .TIF or .TIFF, .JPEG or .JPG, .PICT, and .BMP. (See *GIF* and *JPEG*.)

Firewall
A system of computer hardware and software that isolates a company's local area network from the Internet. The firewall is set up to protect the company's computers from potential tampering from Internet "hackers." Many companies with firewalls contract with Internet service providers to serve their World Wide Web pages.

Flame
An electronic mail message or newsgroup posting that is violently argumentative or intends to attack another user verbally.

FTP
File Transfer Protocol; an Internet tool that allows a user to retrieve and transfer a file from a computer anywhere on the Internet to another computer. FTP files include freeware or shareware programs,

publications, clip art, and many others. The address for FTP sites begins with *ftp*. (See *Anonymous FTP*.)

G

Gateway
A computer that acts as a connector between two physically separate networks. It has interfaces to more than one network and can translate the packets of one network to another possibly dissimilar network.

GIF
Graphic Interchange Format; a type of graphics file format ending with the extension *.GIF* and used extensively on the World Wide Web. (See *File Extension*.)

Gopher
A tool that allows you to search millions of directories and databases of text documents on the Internet through a series of hierarchical menus. Even though most people now use the World Wide Web instead of the gopher, some prefer the faster text-only gopher system. Gopher browsers cannot read World Wide Web pages. The address for Gopher sites begins with *gopher*.

gov
A top-level domain that means government. (See *Domain Extension*.)

Graphical Browser
A special software program, often called a GUI or a graphical user interface and pronounced *gooey*, that allows you to access text, color, video,

sound, and multimedia presentations on the Internet. Popular graphical browsers are Netscape Navigator and Microsoft Internet Explorer.

GUI
See *Graphical Browser*.

H

Home Page
The main page for a World Wide Web site. Often the home page is like an index and has links to other pages at this site. (See *Web Page*.)

Host
An Internet computer.

Hot List
A feature of a graphical browser that lists your bookmarks or favorite pages and allows you to access them quickly and easily. (See *Bookmark* and *Favorites*.)

HTML
HyperText Markup Language; refers to the embedded directions within regular text to create World Wide Web pages. These instructions allow a browser to display a document clearly on your screen. Some HTML documents have *.html* or *.htm* at the end of the URL.

HTTP
HyperText Transfer Protocol; the communications instructions used to connect World Wide Web sites across the Internet. The address for most World Wide Web documents begins with *http*.

Hypertext
A portion of a text document that contains programming code to link a word, graphic,

or phrase to another section in a document or to a different document. Hypertext links on home pages and web pages are highlighted, underlined, or in a different color.

I

Information Superhighway
Also called **cyberspace**; a term popularized by Vice President Al Gore in describing the National Information Infrastructure project. According to his vision, the information superhighway is a high-speed network of computers that will serve thousands of users simultaneously, transmitting e-mail, multimedia files, voice, and video. Its construction is being financed by private industry, primarily the telephone and cable companies. (See *Cyberspace*.)

Internet
Also called *Net*; the worldwide "network of networks" that connects networks to each other using the TCP/IP protocol. Connected networks can transfer files, send electronic mail, exchange newsgroups, and share information via clients such as the World Wide Web, Gopher, and FTP. (See *Client*, *FTP*, *Gopher*, and *World Wide Web*.)

Internet Address
See *E-Mail Address*.

Internet Service Provider
ISP; a company that provides full access to the Internet through a phone line. Many providers are now offering unlimited use dial-up connections to the Internet for reasonable monthly rates. You

must have a computer, communications software, and a modem with a phone line.

J

JPEG
A type of graphics file format (pronounced *jay peg*) ending with the extension *.JPEG* in which photographs are stored for viewing on the World Wide Web. This format compresses the size of a scanned photograph to use less disk space. (See *File Extension*.)

L

LAN
Local Area Network; a group of linked computers located within a specifically defined area such as an office or a building.

Links
See *Hypertext*.

Listserv
Also called a **mailing list**; an electronic discussion group that tends to be more academically focused than newsgroups. A listserv is composed of people who have voluntarily subscribed themselves to focus on a special interest topic. Thousands of listservs exist on all topics. You can join a listserv through your e-mail account.

Login
A procedure to identify yourself to the computer system that provides access to the Internet. Typically, this includes your user ID and password. (See *Logout*.)

Logout
Sometimes referred to as *log-off*; a procedure to inform a computer system that you are quitting your computer session. (See *Login*.)

Lurking
A term that refers to reading but not posting articles to a newsgroup.

Lynx
See *Text Browser*.

M

Mailing List
See *Listserv*.

Microsoft Internet Explorer
See *Graphical Browser*.

mil
A top-level domain that means military. (See *Domain Extension*.)

Modem
The hardware that transfers data by converting computer signals that can be transmitted over a telephone line. Most personal computers come with modems at the speed of 14.4 bps (bits per second) or 28.8 bps. (See *Bits per Second*.)

Multimedia
A combination of more than one medium, such as text, audio, video, graphics, animation, and images.

N

net
A top-level domain that means network provider. (See *Domain Extension*.)

Net
Another term for Internet. (See *Internet*.)

Netiquette
Network etiquette, or the unwritten and written "rules" of etiquette, to be observed when communicating on the Internet.

Netscape Navigator
See *Graphical Browser*.

Network
Two or more computers linked together so that they can exchange files and messages and share resources such as software, hardware, and data. Some large companies and institutions have networks that include thousands of computers.

Newsgroup
See *USENET*.

O

org
A top-level domain that means organization. (See *Domain Extension*.)

P

Password
A secret character string or word used to secure computer systems.

Post
To send or contribute articles to an electronic discussion such as a newsgroup or bulletin board system.

PPP
Point-to-Point Protocol; a type of protocol used to connect a computer to the Internet through a modem and telephone line. Internet service providers usually sell a PPP connection to home users or low-volume individual

business users. PPP is more powerful and dependable than the older SLIP method. (See *SLIP*.)

Protocol
An agreed-upon standard for electronic communications; a common language for computers. This allows users of Apples, PCs, and mainframe computers to communicate with each other over the Internet. (See *TCP/IP*.)

S

Search Engine
An Internet tool that allows you to search for information on a particular topic all across the Internet. After you type a keyword or phrase, the search engine will display documents in which the keyword appears. Popular search engines are Yahoo, AltaVista, Magellan, Lycos, and Excite.

Server
A computer that can provide resources, such as software, hardware, and data, for other computers to use.

Shareware
A method of software distribution in which computer programs are marketed and distributed electronically without proper licensing. The developer may request a registration fee if you decide to keep the software.

SLIP
Serial Line Internet Protocol; a type of protocol used to connect a computer to the Internet through a modem. In most cases, PPP has replaced SLIP. (See *PPP*.)

Snail Mail
A term used to refer to the slower speed of postal mail as contrasted to the faster speed of e-mail.

Subdomain
Each part of a domain. For example, in billg@microsoft.com, *microsoft* and *com* are subdomains in this e-mail address. (See *Domain*, *Domain Name System*, *E-Mail Address*, and *Username*.)

Subscribe
To join or sign up as a member of a newsgroup of listserv. (See *Listserv*, *Unsubscribe*, and *USENET*.)

T

T1 Line
A high-speed, dedicated connection to the Internet that allows hundreds of users to access the World Wide Web server simultaneously.

TCP/IP
Transmission Control Protocol/Internet Protocol; the name of the collection of rules used to connect computers and networks. As a result, one computer can communicate with any other computer on the Internet.

Telnet
The oldest Internet service that allows you to log in to another Internet computer. Telnet is not very common anymore as a means to download information.

TENET
Texas Education Network; a menu-based telecommunications network developed for Texas educators and students

through the Department of Information Resources, the Texas Education Agency, and The University of Texas. TENET provides a communication link to the Internet.

Text Browser
A special software program that provides access to only text (or words) on the Internet. For example, Lynx is a text browser. Lynx does not allow users to view graphics.

U

UNIX
The operating system on many original Internet computers. The UNIX operating system has pieces of basic Internet software built in which allow UNIX users to connect and use the Internet.

Unsubscribe
To cancel membership to a newsgroup or a listserv. (See *Listserv*, *Subscribe*, and *USENET*.)

Upload
To copy a file or information from your computer to another computer or server. (See *Download*.)

URL
Universal Resource Locator; the specific and unique address of a particular document, file, graphic, sound, or video on the World Wide Web.

USENET
Sometimes referred to as Netnews or Usenet News; a network that provides access to electronic discussion groups called newsgroups or conferences. Thousands of newsgroups exist on all topics to

which you can subscribe. With newsgroups you can exchange ideas, ask questions, offer options, or just lurk. The newsgroups to which you have access depend on the service your Internet service provider provides. (See *Internet Service Provider* and *Lurk*.)

Username
Part of an e-mail address that identifies the specific person at the site. For example, in billg@microsoft.com, *billg* is the username. (See *Domain, Domain Name Systems, E-Mail Address,* and *Subdomain*.)

WAIS
Wide Area Information Service; a means to access databases and libraries located on WAIS servers throughout the Internet. WAIS information searches are initiated by keywords and topics and can be compared to the index of a book.

Web Page
Also called **page**; contains the information for a hypertext link. (See *Home Page*.)

White Pages
A term used to reference a database (similar to a telephone book without phone numbers) that contains basic information about subscribers on a network, such as their name, e-mail address, telephone number, and postal address.

WWW
World Wide Web; a hypermedia system that lets you browse through related documents on the Internet through the use of hypertext links. (See *Hypertext*.)

Index